8 Steps to Paying Less for College

A Crash Course in Scholarships, Grants, and Financial Aid

By The Staff of The Princeton Review

PrincetonReview.com

| Penguin
Random
House |

The Princeton Review
110 East 42nd Street, 7th Floor
New York, NY 10017
E-mail: editorialsupport@review.com

Copyright © 2018 by TPR Education
IP Holdings, LLC

ISBN: 978-0-525-56800-1
eBook 978-0-525-56801-8
ISSN: 2578-7659

Editorial
Robert Franek, Editor-in-Chief
David Soto, Director of Content
Development
Danielle Correa, Editor
Stephen Koch, Student Survey
Manager

**Penguin Random House
Publishing Team**
Tom Russell, VP, Publisher
Alison Stoltzfus, Publishing Director
Ellen L. Reed, Production Manager
Amanda Yee, Associate Managing
Editor
Suzanne Lee, Designer

Table of Contents

Get More (Free) Content

1 Go to **PrincetonReview.com/guidebooks**.

2 Enter the following ISBN for your book: 9780525568001.

3 Answer a few simple questions to set up an exclusive Princeton Review account. (If you already have one, you can just log in.)

4 Click the "Student Tools" button, also found under "My Account" from the top toolbar. You're all set to access your bonus content!

Once you've **registered** you can...

- Take a full-length practice SAT.
- Take a full-length practice ACT.
- Get valuable advice about applying to college.

Need to report a **technical** issue?

Contact **TPRStudentTech@review.com** and provide:

- your full name
- email address used to register the book
- full book title and ISBN
- computer OS (Mac/PC) and browser

The **Princeton** Review®

Acknowledgments

This book would not have been possible without the following individuals here at The Princeton Review and beyond: Jen Adams, who was instrumental in the development of this title, and editor Danielle Correa, Scott Harris of Best Content Solutions, and production editor, Melissa Duclos, who transformed the various pieces of the manuscript into the book now in your hands. We'd like to thank Robert Massa, our colleague and friend, for his expertise in financial aid and attention to detail when reviewing the pages of this book. Our continued thanks to our data collection masters David Soto and Stephen Koch for their successful efforts in collecting and accurately representing the statistical data that informs parts of this book.

Most of all, thank you to our readers—we hope this book proves useful in your journey to finding the best financial aid package that suits you and your family. Good luck!

—Rob Franek and The Staff of The Princeton Review

Start Now: Becoming Financially Fit

Introduction

Depending on which survey you read, between 70 and 80 percent of all college-bound high school students were accepted by their first-choice college last year. Except for a handful of schools, selectivity has gone by the board. Nowadays, the problem is not so much getting into college, but paying for it once you are there.

The cost of a four-year private college education has passed the $250,000 mark at some schools, which is enough to cause even the most affluent of parents to want to sit down and cry. The public Ivies—state schools with excellent reputations—have been raising their tuition even faster than the privates. If there is a bright side to all this it is that there is a great deal of financial aid available—and we are talking billions of dollars.

At these prices, almost every family now qualifies for some form of assistance. Many parents don't believe that a family that makes over $150,000 a year, owns their own home, and holds substantial assets could possibly receive financial aid. These days, that family—provided it is presented in the right light—almost certainly does, depending, of course, on the cost of the college in question..

The college financial aid officer (known in college circles as the FAO) is charged with helping the college to enroll students at just the right price.. The FAO does not want to spend more money—or less – than necessary to enroll a student. Let the financial aid officer do his job—believe us, he's very good at it. But in the meantime, you have to do your job, which is to use the rules of financial aid to maximize your eligibility for financial aid and scholarships.

Earnings, assets, and tuition prices aside, one fact trumps all: Parents and students who understand how to apply for financial aid get more financial aid. That said, remember that the primary responsibility for financing an education rests with the family. This book is not about shirking your responsibility. It is about using the need and merit based policies to maximize your eligibility for aid.

So let's be clear: this is not gaming the system. Whether you know it or not, you've been contributing to financial aid funds for years. Each April, you pay federal taxes, a piece of which goes straight to the federal student aid programs. You pay state taxes, part of which goes directly to state schools and to provide grant programs for residents attending college in-state. You may even make contributions to the alumni fund-raising campaign at your own college. You have paid all these years so that someone can get a college education, and now is the time when you can lay claim to some of these funds for your own son or daughter.

10 Financial Aid Myths That Are Holding You Back

You may have heard a lot of myths about paying for college: that's to be expected when you're talking about an act that goes back for centuries. Your father may have had to join the Army to get through state school, and your friend's smart niece may not have even applied to private universities because there was no way her family could afford it. But, as you'll learn in this book, none of that is necessarily true.

1. *Financial strategies are only for rich people*

Many people think that tax loopholes and financial strategy are only for millionaires. In some ways, they have a point: certainly it is the rich who can reap the greatest benefits.

But financial aid strategy is for everyone. Whether you are just getting by or are reasonably well off, you still want to maximize your aid eligibility. Parents who understand the rules get the maximum amount of financial aid they are entitled to under the law. No more, and no less.

2. *The best way to get money for college is through obscure scholarships.*

One commonly accepted myth regarding financial aid is that the best way to get money for school is to search for little-known awards that go unclaimed each year. The reality is that such scholarships represent less than 5 percent of all the aid that is available. The biggest pieces of the financial aid pie comes from private colleges themselves and then from funds provided by the federal and state governments.

3. You won't qualify for aid if you are not a U.S. citizen.

Another myth is that you won't qualify for aid if you are not a U.S. citizen. Certain non-citizens—for example, students who are permanent residents and have a green card—are eligible. In most cases, the parents' citizenship status is actually not relevant at all. And even international students may qualify for funds provided by colleges themselves.

4. Every student at a given college pays the same price.

Going to college is a bit like traveling on an airplane: If you ask the person across the aisle what fare they paid, the answer may be completely different from your own. Some people are paying the full fare for college while others pay far less. That's why you should never initially rule out a school based on "sticker price." What your child ends up paying will depend on what your family can afford and what the school can offer.

5. A school with a lower tuition is always the better deal.

For some families, it many not cost any more to go to a school with a higher tuition than it would to attend one with a relatively inexpensive stated price. While it is true that on average the cost of attending a state institution is less than that of attending a private college or university, depending on a family's income and a college's available aid funds, the cost paid by the family for attending even the most expensive Ivy League schools may be less than the cost of attending an in-state public university. The key is not to focus on the "sticker price," but on how much the family can pay, how much the student has to borrow, and what other kinds of tuition help are available.

6. If you qualify for financial aid, you'll get the same aid from school to school.

While your Expected Family Contribution (EFC) should theoretically be equivalent no matter what school you apply to, what doesn't remain the same is the school. Just like students, each college has different needs and means for who they want to attend, and they can adjust them as such. Schools with deep pockets and similar alumni can afford to offer much more generous aid packages with, for example, lower loans and higher grants than might be available at colleges with smaller endowments.

What also doesn't remain the same is the student—schools that have the leeway to offer greater aid in the form of merit scholarships and other flexible funds will definitely lean towards students that can contribute, whether academically, athletically, or culturally. You may never know the formula behind how a school determines its aid packages, but you can see how much they typically have to award.

7. You get accepted to college first and then you apply for financial aid.

This is perhaps the biggest myth of all! Many, many families believe that you should wait to apply for aid until after your child has been accepted to a college. If you do that, you may well be out of luck. It is crucial to meet financial aid application deadlines—and these deadlines sometimes precede the deadlines for the actual admission application to the college. The Free Application for Federal Student Aid opens every year on October 1—well before regular admission deadlines at most schools.

8. Financial aid is all up to the parents. There's nothing my child can be doing to prepare.

While this book may seem to be addressing the parent or parents, your son or daughter needs to be just as responsible during the process, even if they won't be writing the bulk (or any) of the checks.

We assume that your child is already operating at max capacity in preparing for and applying to college, but they're a huge part of the financial aid process and will have plenty to do as well. Not only do they ultimately have to decide what college to attend (taking into account financial aid offers), they have to apply for scholarships and grants, seek out merit-based awards, and eventually pay off any student loans. They may not be handling the bulk of the financial aid paperwork, but they're in the trenches with you.

9. Financial aid is based solely on my family's finances.

There are so many factors other than (just) a family's assets that determine an aid package—demographics, special talents, academic performance, just to name a few. Any of these factors could make an FAO decide to award merit-based aid or to be more generous in awarding need-based funds. Because colleges give preferential packaging to desirable students, every tenth of a point your child adds to their grade point average or ten points added to their SAT scores may save them thousands of dollars in loans they won't have to pay back later.

Additionally, as far as federal work-study is concerned under the current rules, it makes more sense for students receiving financial aid to earn the minimum amount of money the college will allow, and concentrate on doing as well as possible in school. Most aid is dependent at least in part on the student's grades. A high GPA ensures that the same or better aid package will be available next year; a good GPA also helps students to find better-paying jobs when they graduate so they can pay back their student loans.

10. We'll squeak by for the first year and get more financial aid next year.

No you won't. Colleges rarely increase aid packages unless there as been a significant change in family financial circumstances and even then, an increased award is not guaranteed. Do not accept an admission offer and a financial aid package if you do not have a four-year plan to pay for college given the financial aid awarded for the first year.

.... But don't despair.. We'll give you some helpful strategies to maximize the affordabilty of college in the pages that follow.

Need Based vs Merit-based Financial Aid

While all aid is good aid, there can be conditions attached, and this is more of the school's concern than yours—they must put together a financial package based upon the federal or institutional formula, and figure out from where the money is coming from.

As you might expect, need-based aid is awarded entirely on the financials that the family has submitted, and almost always includes federal grants such as the Pell (for the lowest income students), and state grants and school grants and scholarships that were designated for needy students. With some notable exceptions (such as National Merit), merit-based awards tend to be scholarships awarded by the school or outside entities (which must be reported and often eat into need-based awards).

Keep in mind that each school is pulling from a different pile of money, with various rules assigned. Some schools have lump sums of taxpayer-funded aid or private alumni scholarships that they must assign entirely based on need; others must disburse the funds but can use their discretion. We'll go into this all more in Step 5.

Understanding and Taking Control of the Process

In *8 Steps to Paying Less for College*, we will first give you an overview of the process of applying for aid, and then show you how to begin to take control of that process. We will help you understand what tuition and aid stats are important to look at during the college search, how the college application process should take into account financial aid and "fit", and how to decode your financial aid offer when it arrives. We have devoted an entire chapter (Step Four) to filling out the standardized need analysis forms, because the decisions the colleges will make on the basis of these forms are crucial to your ability to pay for college, as well as a chapter focusing on finding and applying for grants and scholarships. Finally, we'll break down the realities of debt and loans, and offer some creative ways to save money and fund your future.

Your Financial Aid Journey Begins Now

Ideally, you began this process many years ago when your children were quite small. You started saving, at first in small increments, gradually increasing the amounts as your children got older and your earning power grew. You put the money into a mixture of growth investments like stock funds, and conservative investments like treasury bonds, so that now as the college years are approaching you are sitting pretty, with a nice fat college fund, a cool drink in your hand, and enough left over to buy a vacation home in Monte Carlo.

However, if you are like most of us, you probably began thinking seriously about college only a few years ago. You have not been able to put away large amounts of money. Important things kept coming up. An opportunity to buy a home. Taxes. Braces. Soccer camp. Taxes. If your child is already a junior or senior in high school just about to apply for college, don't despair. There is a lot you can do to take control of the process.

A Word of Caution

This book will mainly focus on the financial planning process that takes place in your child's senior year; the interactions with colleges, government agencies, banks, and especially paperwork. When it comes to long-term strategies, there are enough considerations and loopholes to fill a much larger book (such as our own *Paying for College*), and there are individuals who make entire careers out of financial aid consulting. While we strongly recommend sitting down with your accountant or a financial aid consulting service, the next eight chapters should give you an idea of the process as a whole, as well as can't-miss steps and deadlines along the way. Hopefully with this foundation, you'll be able to make smart choices and see the financial aid process with clear, alert eyes. Regardless of where your child is on the road to college, there is something you can be doing to prepare.

Parent's Financial Aid Timeline

Senior Year
August
- Begin gathering all of the prior year returns, forms, and statements you will need for the FAFSA

October 1st
- Filing period for FAFSA and CSS Profile forms opens
- Speak with your child and determine which schools will receive FAFSA/PROFILE data
- Recommended deadline for schools/states that award financial aid on a first come, first served (FCFS) basis

December
- Designate any additional schools to receive FAFSA/PROFILE data in light of early admission/action decisions and regular application intended school changes (see page 59)
- Submit the FAFSA before the end of the calender year, even if your child has not completed the application for admission. An early FAFSA will not be missed in the review process as things heat up in admissions offices later in the spring.

February
- Check with schools and make sure all financial aid forms have been submitted

April/May
- Compare financial aid packages at all your child's accepted colleges, taking into account the total cost of attendance and what it will cost you. DO NOT LOOK JUST AT THE AMOUNT OF THE SCHOLARSHIPS!
- Sign and return financial aid forms on your child's chosen school
- Send any required deposits
- Determine when fees for tuition, room, and board are due
- Make arrangements for health insurance for your child

June 30th
- Last possible date to submit FAFSA (not recommended)

Student Financial Aid Timeline

Freshman/Sophomore Year
- Find out how financial aid can help you afford college
- Learn the basics of college costs
- Get an idea of what college might really cost you and discuss ways to pay for college with your family
- Continue saving money for college

Junior Year
- Learn the difference between sticker price and net price
- Research various types of financial aid
- Think about getting college credit to help you save money
- Research scholarship opportunities
- Look into scholarships that are awarded based on your activities, talents, background, and intended major and see if you qualify
- Get perspective and tips from people you know on paying for college
- Learn about the FAFSA
- Put money to the side that you earned from a summer job
- Working with your parents, gather up all the documents you'll need to fill out your financial aid applications

Senior Year
- Complete your FAFSA with your parents
- Stay on top of priority deadlines for financial aid
- Get an idea of what the colleges on your final list will actually cost by using the Net Price Calculator on each college's website
- Find out about student loans from federal and private sources
- Research local scholarships
- Find out if you need to file a CSS/PROFILE and complete it if required (some of the more selective colleges require this form from the College Scholarship Service in addition to the FAFSA)
- Compare financial aid awards by looking at how much you will have to pay out-of-pocket and how much you will have to borrow.
- If the aid award at the college you wish to attend is not sufficient enough to make your attendance possible, appeal your award by contacting the aid office and asking for additional assistance. Each college will have an appeal process to follow.

- Choose a financial aid package and pay your enrollment deposit at the college of your choice by the deadline
- Contact a college's financial aid office
- Complete financial aid paperwork
- Pay your first college tuition bill

STEP ONE

Learn How Financial Aid Really Works

Let's be honest: most people cannot afford to pay the full cost of four years of college. Financial aid is designed to bridge the gap between what you can afford to pay for school and what the school actually costs. Families that understand how financial aid works come out way ahead.

Let's look at the financial aid process in a nutshell and see how it works. Later on in Step 4, we will take you through each step of this process in greater detail.

What You Can Afford To Pay

Applying for financial aid means filling out forms. A lot of forms.

Need analysis forms are the financial aid applications used to calculate your Expected Family Contribution (EFC). The EFC is the amount of money the family is expected to contribute for the year toward tuition, fees, room, and board, and all the other expenses associated with your student attending college (See more on pg. 15).

The Standardized Need Analysis Forms

FAFSA

At a minimum, you need to fill out a standardized need analysis form called the Free Application for Federal Student Aid (FAFSA). This form, which is available in either a paper, PDF, or online version, can be filled out only after October 1st of the student's senior year in high school. The FAFSA qualifies you for federal aid, but some states and schools use the form to award their own aid as well.

CSS Profile

Many private colleges and some state-supported institutions may require you to electronically complete the CSS Profile form as well for non-federal aid. This form is developed and processed by the College Board, the very same organization that brings you the SAT and AP exams.

Supplemental Forms

A few schools will require other forms as well—for example, selective private colleges often have their own financial aid forms. To find out which forms are required by a particular college, consult the individual school's financial aid office website.

All of the forms ask the same types of prying questions, which would usually earn a gasp at a cocktail party. How much did you earn last year? How much money do you have in the bank? What is your marital status? A hundred or so questions later, the need analysis processing services will have a very clear picture of four things:

- the parents' available income

- the parents' available assets

- the students' available income

- the students' available assets

Expected Family Contribution

After receiving all your financial data, a processing service crunches the numbers to determine your Expected Family Contribution (EFC), or what portion of your income and assets you can afford to put toward college cost of attendance this year:

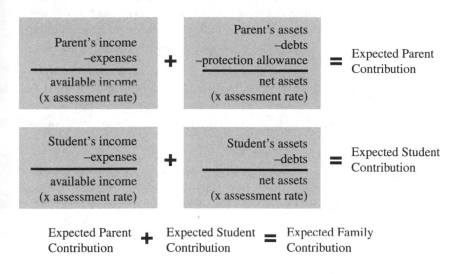

Source: Paying for College, 2019 edition, page 112.

EFC: Federal vs. Institutional Methodology

The processing service for the FAFSA uses a federal formula (called the federal methodology) to calculate your Expected Family Contribution based on your family's income from two tax years prior to the start of the academic year for which you are applying (e.g. if you are applying for the 2019-20 academic year, the income used will be from 2017). This figure will most likely be more than you think you can afford, but remember, that's what parent loans are for.

However, because the federal form does not ask some questions that indicate a family's relative financial strength (such as equity in a home), some schools do not feel that the EFC generated by the FAFSA gives an accurate enough picture of the resources families can draw upon to meet college costs. Using the supplemental information on the CSS Profile (which is analyzed using a formula called the institutional methodology that was developed by the College Board) and/or using their own individual forms, these institutions perform a separate need analysis to determine eligibility for the types of aid that those schools control directly.

In theory, your Expected Family Contribution will be approximately the same no matter what schools your child applies to. Of course, the reality is slightly more complicated. Because some schools are using supplemental data (such as home equity) to determine eligibility for their private aid, your expected contribution at a more selective university will likely be different, and in some cases higher.

What School Costs

The total cost of a year at college, otherwise known as the Cost of Attendance, includes:

- tuition and fees

- room and board

- personal expenses

- books and supplies

- travel

The difference between what you can afford to pay, and the total cost of college is called your "need." Simple, right?

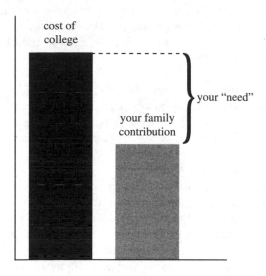

cost of college

your "need"

your family contribution

Source: Paying for College, 2019 edition, page 6

Bridging the Gap: The Financial Aid Package

Meanwhile, the admissions offices of the different colleges have been deciding which students to admit and which to reject. Once they've made their decision, the FAOs step up to the plate. Their job is to put together a package of grants, work-study, and loans that will make up the difference between what they feel you can afford to pay and what the school actually costs.

About the time your child receives an offer of admission from a particular college, you will receive an award letter, which we'll help you decode in Step 6. This letter will tell you what combination of aid the FAO has put together for you in order to meet your need.

The package will consist of three different types of aid:

Grants and Scholarships

These are the best kinds of aid, because they don't have to be paid back. Essentially, a grant is free money. Some grant money comes from the federal government (such as the Pell Grant), some comes from the state, and some comes from the college's wallet itself. Best of all, grant money is almost always tax-free. If you are in the 35 percent combined tax bracket, a $5,000 grant is the equivalent of receiving a raise of $7,692.

Scholarships are also free money, although there may be some conditions attached (academic excellence, for example). Contrary to popular wisdom, scholarships are usually awarded by the schools themselves. The amount of money available from private scholarships outside of a university is actually quite small.

Federal Work-Study (FWS)

The federal government subsidizes this program, which provides part-time jobs to students. The money earned is paid directly to the student who may choose to put the earned funds toward either tuition or living expenses.

Student Loans

These loans are often subsidized (and guaranteed) by state or federal governments. The rates are usually much lower than regular unsecured loans. In most cases, no interest is charged while the student is in school, and no repayment is required until the student has graduated or left college. The largest of these programs is the federal Direct Student Loan. These funds will be included in most financial aid packages, and students do not have to submit a separate application, though they will need to sign a promissory note provided by the college.

Parent Loans

The federal government makes unsecured loans to parents of undergraduates through the PLUS program. Parents may borrow up to the cost of education minus awarded and accepted financial aid. Unlike the federally subsidized Direct Student Loan, the PLUS interest accrues on these loans while the students are in college.

Unmet Need

In some cases, you may find that the college tells you that you have "unmet need." In other words, they were unable to supply the full difference between the cost of their school and the amount they feel you can afford to pay. This is bad news but not atypical, since many colleges do not have sufficient resources to meet the full financial needs of all the students they admit. What the college is telling you is that if your child really wants to attend this college, you will have to come up with even more money than the college's need analysis decided that you could pay.

Usually what this means is that you will have to take on additional debt (see Parent Loans above). If your financial aid offer does include a significant amount of unmet need, we'll cover the possibilities for bridging the gap in Step 7.

Preferential Packaging

The FAOs at the individual colleges have a lot of latitude to make decisions and even to change the figures on the need analysis under strict federal guidelines. After looking at your financial information, for example, they might decide your EFC should be lower or higher than the need analysis computed it originally.

More importantly, the package the FAOs put together for a student will often reflect how much the admissions office wants that student. If a school is anxious to have your child in its first-year class, the package you will be offered will have a larger percentage of grant (free!) money, with a much smaller percentage coming from student loans and work study. If a college is less interested, or if it cannot afford to be competitive, the award will not be as attractive.

Financial Aid for the Academically Gifted

While financial aid is based on your need, it's wise to remember that it is also somewhat on what the colleges need. If the school is truly anxious to get a particular student, it may also sweeten the deal by giving a grant or scholarship that isn't based on need but on merit. A non-need scholarship may actually reduce your family contribution if no federal aid (Pell Grant, Direct Loan, Work Study) is awarded in a package. If there is federal financial aid awarded as part of a need-based package, merit aid must fit within that package which cannot, in combination with other financial aid, exceed your demonstrated financial need.

Raise Your Test Scores, Lower What You Owe

If you've picked up this book in time, consider finding a good test preparation course for the SAT and/or ACT. Several recent studies have shown that coaching can raise a student's SAT score by over 100 points. Again, higher standardized test scores will, at many colleges and universities, increase the value of merit-based scholarships, potentially saving you thousands of dollars and of course, allowing her to apply to more selective colleges. We, of course, are partial to The Princeton Review's in person and online courses and tutors.

The PSAT is the Gateway to Merit Scholarships.

Juniors, get your best possible score on the PSAT. It is the National Merit Scholarship Qualifying Test™ and also used in the selection of students for other scholarships and recognition programs.

When Do you Apply For Financial Aid?

Keep in mind that each school has its own deadlines for financial aid, so you'll want to cross-reference those with the major dates below.

We'll go into the different types of forms in Step 4, but assuming you've filed your taxes for the prior year, the major step in the financial aid game is always going to be completing the Free Application for Federal Student Aid (FAFSA). The FAFSA opens every year on October 1: Think of this as your kickoff event.

If you are applying to private colleges (as well as a few state schools) you may also have to complete the College Board's CSS Profile application.

In addition to the schools' deadlines, some state aid programs or private scholarship programs may have earlier deadlines than the deadlines set by the particular schools for the FAFSA, CSS Profile, and/or their own aid form, and some state agencies award funds on a first come, first served (FCFS) basis. If none of the colleges or your state agency award funds on an FCFS basis, the earliest school's deadline by which a standardized need analysis form must be sent to or received by the need analysis company becomes your overall deadline.

Generally you'll want to file the FAFSA as close to the October 1st opening date as possible, but before your earliest deadline to make sure you are among the first in line to be reviewed once you are admitted.

Let's say your earliest deadline is January 31, 2019 for the 2019–2020 year, but you will be getting a large bonus check from your employer right after New Year's Day for the prior year. You would be better off filing the form before that bonus money inflates your assets. Do you make estimated tax payments? You would be better off making that next payment and have the payment clear your account before you file so that your reportable assets are lower at the time you file. (Confused, yet? Don't worry! We cover high-level tax planning beginning on page 22).

Appealing Your Financial Aid Award

The week acceptance and award letters arrive can be very tough, as you are confronted with the economic realities of the different schools' offers. If the school your child really wants to attend gives you an aid package you cannot accept, you may still be able to negotiate a better deal. If the aid package is actually too low for you to be able to send your child to that school, you have little to lose by asking for more.

When you go back to the table, be sure to know what you want and be able to provide documentation. In some cases, the FAO will alter the aid package enough to make it possible for you to afford to send your child to the school. Later on in Step 6, we'll tell you how to compare award letters, how to appeal your award, and how to apply for the next year.

Same Time Next Year

The need-based financial aid package you accept will last only one year. You will have to go through the financial aid process four separate times in total, filling out a new need analysis form each year until your child reaches the senior year of college. Merit-based awards will typically be renewed annually at the same dollar amount, assuming the student maintains the requisite GPA and enrollment requirements. Make sure you understand these requirements prior to accepting the award and posting your enrollment deposit.

If your financial situation does not vary significantly from year to year, then next year's aid package would probably be very similar to this year's. In some cases, parents' situations do change from year-to-year. In fact, after you finish reading this book, there may be some specific changes you'll want to make.

How College Planning Affects Tax Planning

There are two reasons why tax planning has to change during the college years.

First, the FAOs (unlike the IRS) are concerned about only four years of your financial life. Using a variety of strategies you discuss with your accountant and/or financial aid consultant, you may be able to shift income out of those four years, thus increasing your financial aid.

Second, financial aid formulas differ from the IRS formulas in several key ways. Certain long-term tax reduction strategies (shifting income to other family members, for example) can actually increase the amount of college tuition you will pay. However, astute parents who understand these differences will find that there are some wonderful, legal, logical alternatives they can explore to change the four snapshots the college will take of their income and assets.

Tax accountants who do not understand the financial aid process (and in our experience, this includes most of them) can actually hurt your chances for financial aid.

TIP **Take advantage of education tax benefits.**

A dollar saved on taxes is worth the same as a dollar in scholarship aid. Look into Coverdells, 529 plans, education tax credits, and loan deductions.

The First Base Income Year

Colleges base your ability to pay this year's tuition not on what you made this year; not even on what you made last year; they base it on what you made the year before that, or the Prior-Prior Year (PPY). Thus the first financial aid scrutiny you will undergo will not be directed at the calendar year during which your child will start her first year of college, but two years before. That year is called the first base income year and is the crucial one.

Income vs. Assets

Some parents get confused by what is considered income and what are considered assets. Assets are the money, property, and other financial instruments you've been able to accumulate over time. Income, on the other hand, is the money you actually earned or otherwise received during the past year, including interest and dividends from your assets.

The IRS never asks you to report your assets on your 1040 IRS form—only the income you received from these assets. Colleges, on the other hand, are very interested in your income AND your assets, though they decided long ago that income should be assessed much more heavily than assets. The key to maximizing your financial aid award is reducing the appearance of your assets.

For now, let's focus on income.

Income

When considering their chances for financial aid, many families believe that the colleges are interested only in how much income you make from work. If this were the case, the colleges would just be able to look at your W-2 form to see if you qualified for aid. Unfortunately, life is not so simple. The complicated federal and CSS Profile formulas make the IRS tax code look like a knock-knock joke.

For financial aid purposes, the colleges will be looking at the same income the IRS does. For most of us, that boils down to line 37 of the 1040 form: the Adjusted Gross Income, or AGI (by the way, if you use form 1040A, the AGI is found on line 21; if you use the 1040EZ form, it is on line 4).

But for those who file a tax return, the colleges also look at certain other types of income that are not subject to tax, for example, child support, tax-exempt interest, voluntary contributions to a 401(k) plan or other tax-deferred retirement plan.

Simplified Needs Test

By filing one of the short forms (1040A or 1040EZ), and meeting certain other requirements, you may be able to have parent and student assets excluded from the federal financial aid formulas, which could qualify you for increased federal aid. This is a financial aid loophole known as the "Simplified Needs Test" (SNT).

Here's the way it works at a high level: If the parents have AGI below $50,000 (or are not required to file any personal income tax return), then all your family's assets will be excluded from the federal financial aid formulas. This means that eligibility for the Pell Grant and the subsidized Stafford loan will be determined without regard to how much money the parent or the student has in the bank or in a brokerage account.

It can also be vital to parents with large assets but little real earned income. You can have $49,999 of interest income, and still possibly meet the Simplified Needs Test—in which case even assets of several million dollars will not be used in calculating your federal EFC (this will not be the case at colleges that require the CSS Profile, because these assets cannot be excluded on that form).

The Automatic Zero-EFC

The federal government has a great break for parent(s) in the household who 1) have a PPY combined adjusted gross income of $25,000 or less (or if non-tax filers, have combined income from work of $25,000 or less), and 2) can file the 1040A or the 1040EZ tax form (or are not required to file a tax form at all). Even if your child has substantial income, or you and your child have substantial assets, the student's EFC will be judged to be zero if you meet these requirements.)

> **TIP** **Short Forms Can Be Sweeter**
>
> There may be some financial aid advantages to filling out the short forms (the 1040A or the 1040EZ) if the IRS permits you to do so. And if you are not required to file a personal tax return but still file a 1040 form, you can still be eligible for the Simplified Needs Test or Automatic Zero-EFC.

Assets and Liabilities

Once your available income is listed on the FAFSA and/or the Profile, the next items to disclose are your assets and liabilities. On the standardized financial aid forms, these two items are joined at the hip. Liabilities are subtracted from assets to determine your net assets.

What Counts as an Asset?

Cash, checking and savings accounts, money market accounts, CDs, U.S. Savings Bonds, Educational IRAs, stocks, other bonds, mutual funds, trusts, ownership interests in businesses, and the current market value of real estate holdings other than your home.

None of these items appear directly on your tax return. However, your tax return will still provide the colleges with an excellent way to verify these assets. How? Most assets create income and/or tax deductions, both of which do appear on your 1040 in the form of capital gains, capital losses, interest, dividends, and itemized deductions under schedule A.

Assets in insurance policies and retirement provisions such as IRAs, Keoghs, annuities, and 401(k)s are generally not assessed in the aid. Cars are also excluded from the formula and don't have to be listed on the form.

What About My Home?

Under the federal methodology, the value of your home is not considered part of your assets. This is great news and will help some families who own their own home to qualify for a Pell Grant and other federal aid programs.

However, many highly selective private colleges are using the stricter institutional methodology through the CSS Profile to award their own funds. Under this formula, the value of your home will not be excluded from your assets. If a school asks you to complete the CSS Profile and/or asks you for the value of your home on their own aid form, then most likely the value of the home is going to be treated like other assets. You can bet that the highly selective private colleges that meet a high percentage of their financial aid students' need, will be looking closely at home equity. Other private colleges may or may not.

Assets Are Fleeting, But Financial Aid Lasts...Well, One Year

The need analysis form is a snapshot of your financial situation. The value of most assets (with the exception of money in the bank) changes constantly as financial markets rise and fall. The colleges want to know the value of your assets on the day you fill out the form.

Minimizing the Appearance of Assets

Remember, this is one picture that you don't want to look good for. Trying to appear as fiscally healthy as possible has become almost automatic. However, you have to remember that in applying for financial aid, they aren't going to give it to you if you don't let them see the whole picture, warts and all. On the financial aid form, you don't want to gloss over your debts.

What Counts as a Debt?

The only debts that are considered under the financial aid formulas are debts against the specific assets listed on the aid forms. For example, you do NOT get credit for: unsecured loans, personal loans, educational loans like Direct or PLUS loans for college, consumer debt such as outstanding credit card balances, or auto loans. (We'll cover the different types of student loans in Step 7).

If you have any debt of these types, you should realize that it will NOT be subtracted from your assets under the financial aid formulas. It will be to your advantage to minimize these types of debt during the college years. In fact, you may want to convert these loans into debts that do get credit under the financial aid formulas.

You DO get credit for: margin loans, passbook loans, as well as home equity loans, first mortgages, and second mortgages on "other real estate."

Cash, Checking Accounts, Savings Accounts

The need analysis forms ask you to list any money in your accounts on the day you fill out the forms. However, you can't list this money if it isn't there.

We are not counseling you to go on a spending spree, but if you were planning to make a major purchase in the near future, you might as well make it now. If you were going to replace the boiler, if you can prepay your summer vacation, if you were going to buy a new car sometime in the next year, do it now, and pay cash. You were going to make these purchases anyway. By speeding up the purchase, you reduce the appearance of your cash assets. If you were going to buy soon, buy now and use cash.

One word of caution. The more you spend now as a strategy to maximize your aid eligibility, the more you will need to depend on a college's willingness to offer financial aid rather than on your own ability to finance your child's education. That may be a good strategy if your student is highly competitive for admission at the college of his dreams, but it could backfire if your student is seeking admission to a highly competitive college that may not look too kindly on your choice to prepay your summer vacation, for example.

Paying Off Your Plastic Debt

If you have credit card debt, your need analysis form won't give a realistic picture of your net worth, because as far as the needs analysis formulas are concerned, plastic debt simply means you are choosing to live beyond your means. You could owe thousands of dollars on your VISA card, but the aid formula does not allow you to subtract this debt from your assets, or to subtract the interest on the debt from your income. By paying off credit card debt with money in the bank, not only do you reduce interest paid to the credit card company, you reduce your net assets on the need analysis form and pick up some more aid.

Your Tax Bill

If you did not have enough tax withheld from your wages this year, and you will end up owing the IRS money, consider speeding up the completion of your taxes so that you can send in your return—with a check—before you complete the need analysis form. If you are self-employed, you might consider prepaying your next quarterly estimate to reduce your reportable cash assets.

Timing on IRA Contributions

The IRS allows you to make contributions to an IRA from January 1st of one year through April 15th of the following year. It makes sense to make retirement provisions as soon as possible in a calendar year; not only will you shelter the money itself from assessment as an asset but you will also shelter the interest earned by that money: If you leave that money in a regular bank account for most of the year, the interest will have to be reported on the need analysis form as regular income. By making the contribution early in the year, the interest earned by that contribution will be out-of-bounds to the needs analysis formulas.

Asset Protection Allowance

After the FAFSA or Profile processor has determined your net assets, there is one final subtraction, called the Asset Protection Allowance.

This number, based on the age of the older custodial parent (or custodial step-parent), is how much of your net assets can be exempt from the federal financial aid assessment. The older you are, the more assets are sheltered. The chart on the following page will give you a rough idea of the asset protection allowance permitted at various ages under the federal methodology. According to the Department of Education, this allowance is calculated to yield the same amount of money as "the present cost of an annuity which, when combined with social security benefits, would provide at age 65 a moderate level of living for a retired couple or single person." Of course, their idea of "a moderate level of living" probably doesn't involve as many indulgences as you'd prefer.

After subtracting the asset protection allowance, the remaining assets are assessed on a sliding scale (depending on income). The maximum assessment on parents' assets is 5.65 percent. In other words, the most you will have to contribute is slightly more than five and a half cents for each additional dollar of assets.

Assets and Liabilities: How the Methodologies Differ	
The Federal Methodology	**The Institutional Methodology**
• Does not assess home value • Does not assess farm value provided the family lives on the farm and can claim on Schedule F of the IRS 1040 that they "materially participated in the farm's operation" • Does not assess business net worth for a "family business" provided your "family" owns and controls more than 50 percent of the business and it has 100 or fewer full-time (or full-time equivalent) employees • Asset protection table based on present cost of an annuity • Provides for exclusion of all assets if you meet the Simplified Needs Test • Asset assessment on a sliding scale based in part on income	• Assesses home value, but some colleges will choose to ignore home equity (though sometimes only if family income is below a certain threshold) or cap home value at 2.4 times income or cap home equity at 2 times income • Assesses all farm equity and all business equity • All assets are assessed, regardless of whether or not you meet the simplified needs test • Asset assessment is unrelated to income, except for those with negative available income • Assets held in names of siblings considered as parental assets • Asset allowances based on emergency reserves, educational savings, and low-income supplements)

Student Resources

The FAFSA and Profile ask precisely the same questions about students' income and assets that they do about the parents' income and assets, but there is one major difference in the way students' money is treated. The formula takes a much larger cut of students' money.

In the federal formula, a student's assets are assessed at a breathtaking rate of 20 percent each year (versus a ceiling of 5.65 percent on parents' assets). In the institutional (Profile) formula, for the past few years, the assessment rate has been 25 percent. A student's income under the federal formula is assessed at up to 50 percent (versus a ceiling of 47 percent on parents' income). The current assessment rates have set up a bizarre situation, in which the best way a student receiving financial aid can help his parents pay for college is by not working very much (unless, of course, the college will expect a minimum contribution of summer savings from every student, whether they choose to work or not – and many selective private colleges do just that, regardless of what the needs analysis formula might yield).

Student Income: Federal Methodology

Under the federal formula, there is no minimum contribution from student income, and the first $6,570 (after tax) dollars earned by a dependent student are excluded.

Thus an incoming first year student can earn about $7,200 before he will be assessed one penny. Once he crosses the $7,200 threshold, his additional income will most likely be assessed at a rate of 50 percent. If he then saves his money, it will also be assessed as an asset at a rate of 20 percent. Thus, if he banks his 7,201st

> **TIP** **Students, don't work too much.**
>
> For a student who hopes to receive aid from a school using only the federal methodology, it doesn't make sense to have income higher than $7,200.
>
> For a student who hopes to receive aid from a school using the institutional methodology, it doesn't make sense to have income higher than $4,708 as a first-year student, or $6,238 as an upperclassman.

dollar, 50 cents of it will be assessed as income and 20 cents of it will be assessed as an asset. The extra dollar he earned could cost him 70 cents in reduced aid.

Student Income: Institutional Methodology

If your child attends a private college that uses the institutional methodology, she may be responsible for a minimum first-year contribution as high as $2,000 ($2,650 as an upperclassman) and there is no $6,570 income protection allowance. A student at a private college will owe no more than the minimum contribution as long as she keeps her income below $4,708 as a first-year and $6,238 as an upperclassman. Over $4,708, she may be losing 71 cents in aid eligibility on each additional dollar she earns and saves.

Putting It All Together

Parents always want the bottom line. "How much will I have to pay?" they ask, as if there were one number fixed in stone for their family. As you go through the aid process, you will see as you begin to play with your numbers that there are numerous ways to present yourselves to the colleges. Your bottom line will also be determined in part by whether you choose schools that use the federal or the institutional methodology to award institutional aid.

By using some of the financial strategies we have outlined and even deeper ones discussed with your accountant or financial aid consultant, you can radically change the financial snapshot that will determine your Expected Family Contribution.

STEP TWO

Sticker Shock: Understanding College Costs

Because colleges have different policies on meeting full need, how they put together an aid package and what they consider to be the cost of education beyond direct charges (e.g. books and personal expenses), financial aid offers often differ by many thousands of dollars between schools, particularly selective ones.

We would be suspicious of counselors who say they can predict the precise amount and type of aid you will receive from a school. Applying for college is something of a financial crapshoot, and the best you can do is know how to play all of the cards in the deck.

What Does College Really Cost?

We've said it before, and we'll say it again: you should never initially rule out a school based on "sticker price." Other than at the most selective private and public colleges, very few families pay full price for college. The actual cost of attendance can vary wildly, even for families that might appear economically similar on the surface. A generous aid award from a pricey private school can make it less costly than a public school with a lower sticker price.

College Costs Can Vary

The end result of college—that is, a degree—may be the same, but there is nothing standard about the monetary units it takes to get there. This will be most obvious in the tuition between state and private schools, but as you get further in to planning, other price differences will become more apparent. Room and board also might appear to be a clear-cut line item, but if you look at the school's housing policies and trends, you may find that the vast majority of students tend to live off campus as upperclassmen, and the cost of living in the area isn't so bad (plus, your child gets the whole ramen experience).

Why The "Sticker Price" Doesn't Necessarily Matter

Don't initially rule out any school as being too expensive based on the price tag; it's the portion of that price that you actually have to pay that counts. In theory, your EFC will be approximately the same no matter what schools your child applies to.

	School A State School	School B Ivy League School
Tuition	$25,300	$70,000
Your EFC	$20,300	$20,300
Aid Package	$5,000	$49,700

If your EFC is calculated to be $20,300 and your child is accepted at a state school that costs $25,300, you will pay about $20,300, and the school will make up the difference—in this case $5,000—with an aid package. If you apply to a prestigious Ivy League school that costs $70,000, you will still pay about $20,300 and the school will make up the difference with an aid package of approximately $49,700.

Net Price vs "Sticker Price"

The net price that a family actually pays for college will almost certainly be lower than the sticker price; it's the first number you'll consider once all of the aid is taken into account. After all the time you spend filling out forms, you'd think that the EFC would finally give you the answer to the question of "How much will we pay?" It is a bit more complicated than that because the EFC represents the current "out-of-pocket" contribution your family is expected to make. Work study, where the student earns money to help defray the cost of education and loans where the student (and many times the parent as well) will be paying from future earnings, also represent direct costs to you. Only grant or scholarship money provide a real discount from the list price. The award letter should let you know the total cost of attendance, including estimates for books, travel and personal expenses. It should subtract the EFC from that cost of attendance, and it should provide a financial aid package consisting of scholarships, grants, loans and work to make up the difference. But as we said earlier, many colleges, especially public colleges and less selective private schools, will not always meet the full need (Cost of Attendance minus EFC). The aid package is like a little city of financial neighborhoods: grants, scholarships, work-study opportunities. Some—such as grants—will be free money, and some will be amounts the student will be expected to pay. There are going to be some costs that are variable (like travel) and some that are etched in stone (like tuition)—just know that in the same way the sticker price is not hard and fast, the net price isn't, either.

The Cost of a Private College

According to the College Board, the average cost of a year's tuition, room and board, and fees at a private college during the 2016-17 school year was $45,370. Many experts predict that the cost of private college will increase at a rate of about 3.5 percent per year. Here is a chart of what the average cost of a year of private college would be over the next 15 years, based on 3.5 percent yearly growth:

Average Annual Cost of a Private College in	
2018: $48,593 (today)	2026: $63,989
2019: $50,294	2027: $66,229
2020: $52,054 (2 years)	2028: $68,547 (10 years)
2021: $53,876	2029: $70,946
2022: $55,762	2030: $73,429
2023: $57,714 (5 years)	2031 $75,999
2024: $59,724	2032: $78,659
2025: $61,825	2033: $81,412 (15 years)

*Source: Paying for College, 2019 edition, page 18

Of course, if your child decides on one of the most prestigious private schools, the cost will be even more. In 2018, most of the top colleges crossed the $65,000-a-year barrier. In five years, at 3.5 percent growth per year, that will be approximately $77,200.

The Cost of a Public University

The average cost of a year's tuition, room and board, and fees at a public university during the 2016-17 school year was $20,090 (according to the College Board). Many experts predict that the cost of public university will also increase at a rate of about 3.5 percent per year over the next decade. Here is a chart of what the average cost of a year of public university could cost over the next 15 years, if the experts are right:

Average Annual Cost of a Public University in	
2018: $21,393 (today)	2026: $27,098
2019: $22,025	2027: $27,911
2020: $22,696 (2 years)	2028: $28,748 (10 years)
2021: $23,376	2029: $29,610
2022: $24,077	2030: $30,498
2023: $24,799 (5 years)	2031: $31,413
2024: $25,543	2032: $32,355
2025: $26,309	2033: $33,325 (15 years)

Source: Paying for College, 2019 edition, page 19

Of course, if you are attending one of the "Public Ivies" (such as the University of Virginia) as an out-of-state resident, the cost is already close to $61,994. In five years, at a 3.5 percent growth rate per year, that would be close to $73,626. Flip to Step 3 to learn more about the Public Ivies.

How Much Will You Need?

If your child is fifteen, ten, or even five years away from college, they probably not even begun to think about what kind of school to attend. Since you can't ask your child, ask yourself: What kind of college could you picture your son or daughter attending?

If you have picked a private college of average cost, and your child is ten years away from college, look up the price on the first chart we gave you above. Rather than concentrating on the cost of freshman year, look at the cost of junior year, two years further on. Whatever this number is, multiply it by four. This is a rough approximation of an average college education at that time.

If you picked an average public university, and your child is five years away from college, look up the price on the second chart above. Count two years more and multiply that number by four. This is a rough approximation of a college education at an average public university at that time. Of course, if costs increase faster than the experts are projecting, the figure could be more.

If you wish to be even more precise, find a guide to colleges and look up the current price of a particular school you are interested in. Let's choose Spelman College, a Historically Black College for women, which has a current price of about

$40,110, and let's say your daughter is going to be ready to go to college in five years. Multiply the current price by our assumed rate of increase:

$$\$41,514 \times 1.035 = \$42,967$$

The new number is the price of that school next year. To find out the projected price of Spelman in five years, just repeat this operation four more times ($42,967 × 1.035 = $44,471; $44,471 × 1.035 = $46,027; etc.). For ten years, repeat the operation nine more times.

Of course, these will only be rough estimates since no one has a crystal ball. If your daughter were to start Spelman five years from now, the first year would cost roughly $49,305. By the time she is a junior, the projected cost would be $52,817. To figure out the grand total, multiply the cost of junior year by four. This is a rough projection of the cost of a four-year education.

At Spelman five years from now, a college education will cost about $211,270. At Stanford or Yale, the bill will most likely exceed $325,000.

Now, don't faint just yet. This is a great deal of money, but:

1.   Financial aid will help lower your out-of-pocket expenses

2.   You still have time to plan, save, and invest

3.   Your earning power will most likely increase over time

The Rise of "Free" Tuition

A few states have offered free community college tuition for some time—but in the spring of 2017, New York became the first state to offer free tuition for up to four years of college for full-time students attending public colleges in the state from family incomes under $120,000, with the caveat that they remain and work in New York State for at least four years after graduation. More states followed suit and will continue to do so. It's important to understand that going to these schools is by no means free. For example, in New York, this offer only covers tuition, not room and board, books, etc. And at most state universities, it turns out that room and board expenses are higher than the tuition itself.

Be aware that there may be balls of string attached to such awards—be sure to read all the fine print about qualifying and maintaining eligibility for such funds, as well as any requirements that must be met after leaving school.

When to Begin Saving/Investing

Now that you know a little bit about college costs and the financial aid process, let's talk about actually getting started.

And the important thing is to get started. It is easy to get so paralyzed by the thought of the total cost of a four-year college education that you do nothing. The important thing is to begin saving something as early as possible as regularly as possible—even if you haven't done any early planning and college is right around the corner. It doesn't matter if you can't contribute large amounts. The earlier you start, the longer you give your money to work for you. If you have not saved the total cost of four years' tuition at a private college (and very few parents ever have), you are not alone. Most families haven't. And that is part of the reason why there is financial aid.

Will Saving For College Hurt My Financial Aid Chances?

In other words, why bother saving at all? Won't one just get more financial aid? Trust us, you will be much better off if you save for college. A family without the means to pay for college will find concerned financial aid officers ready to look in every corner of their coffers to come up with the aid necessary to send that family's child to college. An affluent family that has lived beyond their means for years and is now looking for the college to support this lifestyle with financial aid will find the FAOs (financial aid officers at the colleges) to be very unsympathetic and tightfisted. These men and women have broad powers to increase or decrease your family contribution; to allocate grants; to meet your family's entire need—or just part of it. An honest attempt to save money and a willingness to make sacrifices can make a large impression on the FAOs. Provided they are placed in the proper types of accounts, additional funds in a parent's name have only a minor impact on aid eligibility.

If you still aren't convinced, think about this: A proportion of the financial aid package can come in the form of loans. You have the choice of saving now and earning interest or borrowing later and paying interest. Earning interest is more fun. Besides, money in the bank gives you options. A college fund, even a small one, gives you control over your own destiny. What if the college your child really wants to attend doesn't fully meet your need? What if you lose your job just as the college years are approaching? By planning a little for the future now, you can ensure that you'll have options when the college years are upon you.

How Much Should We Save Every Month?

Any realistic long-term plan is more of an educated guess than an exact prediction. There are so many unknown factors—how much will college cost in ten years? What will the inflation rate average over the next decade? Will stocks continue to be the best long-term investment as they have been for the past forty years, or will some unforeseen trend make real estate or bonds a better investment?

Any financial planner who says you have to save an exact amount per month to reach your goal is being unrealistic—in part because you don't even know with certainty what that goal will be. The important thing is to start. It doesn't matter if you can't contribute large amounts. The earlier you start, the longer you give your investments to work for you.

The Joys of Compound Interest

Let's say that you had a pretty good year this year and were able to save $4,000. You invest this money in a high-yield mutual fund. Some of these funds have been averaging a return of over 8 percent a year, but let's be more conservative and say you got a 7 percent rate of return, which you plow back into the fund. Don't like mutual funds? That's fine. This is just an example to show you how investments grow. To find out how much $4,000 would earn in one year at 7 percent, multiply $4,000 times 1.07.

$$\$4,000 \times 1.07 = \$4,280$$

To find the value of the investment over five years, repeat this calculation four more times ($4,280 × 1.07 = 4,580; $4,580 × 1.07 = $4,900; etc.) In five years, your original $4,000 will be worth $5,610. In ten years, it will have grown to $7,869. Not bad, especially when you consider that this comes from only one year of saving.

Of course, this example is a little simplified. One or two of those years might be bad years and the fund might not pay 7 percent. Other years might be extremely good years and the yield could be much higher. There are tax implications to consider as well. However, $7,869 is a reasonable forecast of what one $4,000 investment could be worth in ten years.

And if you continued to invest another $4,000 each year for the next ten years, with the same rate of return—well, now we're talking real money. At the end of ten years, you would have a college fund in excess of $59,134.

Timing of Investments

Because of the way compounding works it would be better, in theory, to make your largest contributions to a college investment fund in the early years when the investment has the most time to grow. Unfortunately the reality of the situation is that a couple just getting started often doesn't have that kind of money.

If you get a windfall—an inheritance, a large bonus, a year with a lot of over-time—by all means put that money to work for you. However, for most parents, it will be a matter of finding the money to invest here and there.

Types of Investments

The key to any investment portfolio is diversity. You will want to spread your assets among several different types of investments, with varying degrees of risk. When your child is young, you will probably want to keep a large percentage of your money in higher-risk investments in order to build the value of the portfolio. As you get closer to the college years, it is a good idea to shift gradually into less volatile and more liquid investments. By the time the first year of college arrives, you should have a high percentage of cash invested in short-term treasuries, CDs, or money market funds.

Here is a high-level look at some of your investment options. We go into the intricacies of each option, along with more advantages and potential drawbacks, in *Paying for College*.

Stock Mutual Funds

Rather than buying individual stocks, you can spread your risk by buying shares in a mutual fund that manages a portfolio of many different stocks. Most newspapers and financial magazines give periodic rundowns of the performance of different mutual funds. The minimum investment in mutual funds varies widely, but often you can start with as little as $1,000. In general, we recommend no-load or low-load funds that charge a sales commission of 4.5 percent or less.

High-Yield Bonds

Another aggressive investment to consider is high-yield bonds, which pay a high rate of interest because they carry a high level of risk. The best way to participate in this market is to buy shares in a high-yield bond fund. The bonds are bought by professionals who presumably know what they are doing, and again, because the fund owns many different types of bonds, the risk is spread around.

Normal-Yield Bonds

If you want less risk, you might think about buying investment-grade bonds (rated at least AA) which can be bought so that they mature just as your child is ready to begin college. If you sell bonds before they mature, the price may vary quite a bit, but at maturity, bonds pay their full face value and provide the expected yield, thus guaranteeing you a fixed return.

EE Savings Bonds

If you don't earn too much money, Series EE Savings Bonds offer an interesting option for college funds as well. The government a few years ago decided that if an individual over 24 years of age with low to moderate income purchases EE Savings Bonds after 1989 with the intention of using them to pay for college, the interest received at the time of redemption of the bonds will be tax-free. EE Savings Bonds are issued by the federal government, and are as safe as any investment can be. They can also be purchased in small denominations without paying any sales commission. However, EE Savings Bonds have several drawbacks—one is their low rate of return—so do you research before jumping in.

Tax-Free Municipal Bonds

Those families that are in the 25 percent income tax bracket (or higher) may be tempted to invest in tax-free municipal bonds. As usual, you can reduce your risk by buying what is called a tax-free muni fund. These come in different varieties, with different degrees of risk. One thing to be aware of is that while the IRS does not tax the income from these investments, the colleges effectively do. Colleges call tax-exempt interest income "untaxable income" and assess it just the way they assess taxable income.

Trusts

Establishing a trust for your child's education is another way to shift assets and income to the child. Trusts have all the tax advantages of putting assets in the child's name—and then some; they allow more aggressive investment than do custodial accounts; they also give you much more control over when and how your child gets the money. The drawbacks of trusts are that they are initially expensive to set up, costly to maintain, and very difficult to change—more important, they also jeopardize your chances of qualifying for financial aid because the formulas expect a much higher percentage of student assets to go toward college expenses than they do for parental assets.

529 Plans

Forty-nine states—all except Wyoming—and the District of Columbia now offer special programs that are designed to help families plan ahead for college costs. These Qualified State Tuition Programs, which are more commonly called Section 529 plans (after the relevant section of the Internal Revenue Code), come in two basic forms: tuition prepayment plans and tuition savings accounts. Most states offer one type or the other, but a number of states offer or will soon offer both. Some plans have residency requirements for the donor and/or beneficiary. Others (like California) will allow anyone to participate. While some states limit who can contribute funds to the plan (usually the parents and grandparents), other states have no such restrictions. Funds from 529 plans will reduce your demonstrated financial need for assistance, but they give you enormous flexibility in selecting the right college for your child.

Coverdell ESAs

While contributions to these special educational savings accounts are not tax deductible, any withdrawals used for post-secondary education will be totally tax-free. While there are income limits that affect your ability to contribute to such an account—the law does not specify that contributions must be made by the beneficiary's parents. Other relatives or even friends who fall below the income cutoffs could presumably contribute.

It's Not Only About Saving for College

Remember to invest in other things besides your child's college education. Providing a college education for your child is probably not the only ambition you have in life. During the years you are saving for college you should not neglect your other goals, particularly in two important areas: owning your own home (which we have just spoken about) and planning for your retirement.

Home Ownership

In addition to saving and investing, a supplementary method to fund college can involve owning your own home. If you can swing it, owning your own home is a top priority in any plan for paying for college. Equally important, building equity in your home provides you with collateral you can use to help pay for college. Finally, owning your home provides you with an investment for your own future, which you should never lose sight of. When the kids rush off to embark on their own lives, clutching their diplomas, will there be something left for you? What good is a college education for the child if it puts the parents in the poorhouse? Your home can be a particularly valuable kind of college fund. The federal government and most colleges do not consider home equity in one's primary residence when determining aid eligibility. Generally, the more equity you have in your home, the more you can borrow against it. And even if your child attends a school that assesses home equity when awarding their own aid funds, should you borrow against your home you'll reduce your total assets in the eyes of the FAOs, which can reduce how much you have to pay for college.

Planning for Retirement

While the colleges assess your assets and income, they generally don't assess retirement provisions such as Individual Retirement Accounts (IRAs), 401(k) plans, Keoghs, tax-deferred annuities, etc. Any money you have managed to contribute to a retirement provision will be off-limits to the FAOs at most schools. Thus contributions to retirement plans will not only help provide for your future but also will shelter assets (and the income from those assets) from the FAOs. In addition, many employers will match contributions to 401(k) plans, in effect doubling your stake. And let's not forget that, depending on your income level, part or all of these contributions may be tax-deferred.

STEP THREE

Craft Your College List

Now that you understand how financial aid works, let's look at how you and your family can choose colleges with financial aid in mind. If you've never heard of a "financial safety school," then this chapter's for you!

Many factors go into a decision to apply to a specific college—campus culture, academics, career development. One factor that cannot be ignored is money. You and your child are about to make a business decision, and it's vital that you keep a clear head.

Price is not always synonymous with quality; it is possible to pay $46,000 per year for a college that is a poor fit for your child, and $7,000 per year for a college that fits them like a glove. The real determining factor is the education the student comes away with and how seriously the student intends to take the experience.

Crucial College Conversations

Communication is the most critical part of this process. Parents and students serve as reality checks for each other. Will you be paying for everything, or will your child carry some of the burden? While you don't need to go into the minute details of your finances, it is a good idea to tell your child what you can really afford.

While you're at it, think (and talk about) what it is you want for your child in their college experience. As a parent, are you looking only at schools with very high admission standards? Make sure you're working with your student to select at least one college with a high acceptance rate where your student's standardized test scores and GPA are above the average for the typically admitted student. A good college with a high acceptance rate where your child has above average grades and scores is likely to award higher scholarship and grant awards than a more selective school where your child's scores are below the average.

You may also come to realize that you and your child have differing expectations about college. You might want your son to attend school near home, while he actually wants to go to school three states away. Your daughter may want to major in literature, while you've always thought she would be an engineer. Although you may suspect that you know best, please take some extra time to consider the incredible opportunity—and daunting challenge—that this period of time presents to your child as a young person on the brink of adulthood.

How to Pick Colleges with Financial Aid in Mind

One of the frustrating parts about applying to college is that you have to apply without really knowing what you're going to end up paying. Of course you know the sticker price, but as we've already said many a time, the many families don't actually pay the sticker price. The $64,000-a-year question is what kind of aid package the different schools will give you to reduce that sticker price.

1. Look Beyond the Ivy League

We aren't suggesting that Ivy League schools aren't worth it, or that your child should not apply to them, but it is worth noting (even as you look at that $64,000 price tag) that many important, interesting people have managed and still are managing to get good educations elsewhere—and for less money.

2. Remember: This Is a Joint Decision With Your Child

Many parents feel that it is somehow their duty to shield their children from harsh economic realities. They allow their children to apply to any school they like, without thinking through the consequences of what an acceptance at that school would mean.

> **TIP** **Money Talks**
>
> If money is a consideration, discuss this openly with your child. Look at the relative merits and eventual outcomes of the schools as compared to their price tags, and discuss what sacrifices both the parent and the student would have to make in order to send the student to one of the more expensive schools if the aid package you get is low.

Taking on large amounts of debt should be a rational rather than an emotional decision, and any important decision like this should involve the student as well. Especially if money is a concern, your child should be included in every step of the decision making, from computing a rough estimate of your family's Estimated Family Contribution (EFC) to picking schools for their college list, with a view toward financial aid.

3. Apply to More Schools

One good offer can frequently lead to others. If you have received a nice package from school A, you can go to comparable school B that your child is more interested in, and ask them to reconsider for an improved package based upon the other school's offer.

For this reason, students who need financial aid should always apply to a variety of colleges every one of which the student would be happy to attend. Perhaps one or two of these should be "reach" schools at which the student is qualified but less certain of admission. The student should also apply to several schools that not

---

How Many Schools Should You Apply To?

At The Princeton Review, we recommend choosing six schools:

- Two dream schools (or "reach" schools)

- Two match schools (where you'll probably, but not necessarily, be accepted)

- Two safety schools (you and your counselor are very confident you'll be accepted, and be able to afford tuition)

You can adjust this number up or down as needed, but you should apply to at least one school in each category, and you don't need to apply to ten or more schools.

*Adapted from *College Admission 101: Simple Answers to Tough Questions about College Admissions and Financial Aid* by Robert Franek, America's Leading College Expert from The Princeton Review

---

only fit his academic profile but also have good reputations for meeting students' full "financial need". Finally, the student should apply to what we call a "financial safety school," which we'll explain in just a bit.

4. Don't Be Modest

In many cases, schools themselves select the recipients for scholarships and grants based on admissions materials, with a keen eye toward enticing high-caliber students to their programs. It is therefore crucial that the student sing their own praises in every aspect of the application, from essays right down to suggesting topics for teachers to include in their letters of recommendation.

5. Think About Aid Sustainability

It is also vital to make sure that there is a reasonable expectation that the aid package will be available for the next three years as well. How high do the student's grades have to be in order to keep the package intact? Are any of the grants or scholarships they gave you one-time-only grants? Once you've received an offer, check the fine print in the award letter and ask these questions of the financial aid officer.

What Stats Are Important?

If you are selecting a private college with financial aid in mind, there are some criteria you should research as you look at the colleges:

- What is the average percentage of need met (remember, Need = Total Cost of Education – Expected Family Contribution)? You can find this statistic in most college guides. A high percentage is a sign that the school is committed to meeting as much of a student's "need" as possible; however, keep in mind this is an average. A school that normally meets only a low percentage of need may come through with a spectacular offer for a student the school really wants. Another school that normally meets a very high percentage of need may make a very low offer to a student the school considers marginal.

- Does the student have something this particular school wants? Even at the most prestigious schools, where students are awarded aid based only on their "need," applicants with high academic achievement do get preferential packaging—award packages with a higher percentage of grants and a lower percentage of loans.

- Other factors that can sway an award package your way: Is the student a legacy? Is he an athlete applying to a school known for that division I or II sport? Is she a chemistry genius applying to a school known for the strength of its chemistry department?

- How does the student compare to last year's incoming class test score and GPA averages? If this is a reach school for the student, the aid package may not be outstanding. Some colleges (particularly public ones) are very open about their academic wants; they mention right up front in their promotional literature that a student with SAT scores above x and a GPA of above y will receive a scholarship worth z.

- What percentage of gift aid is NOT based on need? If a student has an excellent academic record, this statistic might give some indication of whether she will be eligible to receive non-need scholarships. Of course, this statistic might be misleading for the same reasons we mentioned above.

- What is the school's endowment per student? If the school is on its last legs financially, then it may not be able to offer a great aid package. Don't necessarily be scared if a small school has a small endowment—take a closer look at what that actually means. A school could have a relatively small endowment, but a very high endowment per student.

- Will the school use the institutional methodology from the College Scholarship Service in awarding aid under the school's direct control? Recall that unlike the federal formula, CSS considers home equity and a few other enhancements to income and assets that lower need. Many colleges that use the institutional methodology often tweak the formula; for example, making adjustments for the cost of living for those families residing in high cost areas.

Federal vs. Institutional Methodologies

By now you might have figured out that in many cases the federal methodology is kinder on a parent's pocketbook than the institutional methodology. However, before you start looking only at schools that use the federal methodology, there are a number of points to be made:

1. A college that uses the institutional methodology must still award federal money such as the Pell Grant and the subsidized Direct loan using the federal criteria. Thus, the institutional methodology will only affect funds under the institution's direct control—principally, the school's private grant money.

2. Families may find that the difference in aid packages from two schools using the different methodologies is actually not very significant. Families who don't have a lot of equity built up in their primary residence, who don't show business or capital losses, or losses on property rental, may not notice much difference at all.

3. Most of the competitive schools will be using the institutional methodology to award the funds under their control. It would limit your choice of colleges to apply only to schools that use the federal methodology.

 TIP The best way to find out which methodology is being used is to ask an FAO at that school. However, as a rough guide: if the school wants you to fill out the CSS PROFILE form, then it will be using the institutional methodology.

The Financial Safety School

Look, your child just may well get into her dream school. Just as important, that dream school may give her an acceptable financial aid package. However, part of picking colleges entails selecting second, third, fourth, and fifth choices as well, from both an admissions and financial aid perspective.

Just as it is important to select a safety school where your child is likely to be accepted, it is also important to select what we call a "financial safety school" that is affordable out-of-pocket in the event that the more expensive schools you applied to do not provide enough aid to make your enrollment possible. There are three factors to take into account when picking a financial safety school.

1. The Student is Pretty Much Guaranteed to Get In. What is an admissions safety school for one student may be a reach for another. Force yourself to be logical. A good way to figure out a student's chances for admission is to look up the median SAT and ACT scores and class ranking of last year's freshman class. A particular college qualifies as a safety school if the student applying is in the top 25 percent of the students who were admitted to the college last year.

2. You Can Afford To Attend Even if You Received No Aid at All.

For most families, of course, this means some sort of state or community college. There are some excellent public colleges, whose educational opportunities rival those of many of the best private colleges.

3. The Student is Happy to Attend.

We've met some students who freely admit they wouldn't be caught dead going to their safety school. As far as we are concerned, these students either haven't looked hard enough to find a safety school they would enjoy, or they have unreasonable expectations about what the experience of college is supposed to be.

What Counts as a Financial Safety School?

Let's examine what you might be looking for in a financial safety school based on a rough approximation of your EFC.

If You Have Extremely High Need

If your EFC is in the $700 to $5,000 range, a good safety school would be a public university or community college located in your own state. This type of school has two advantages. First, the likelihood that you will be eligible for state aid is extremely good. Second, your child may be able to live at home and commute and save most of the expenses of room and board.

However, a student with high need should not neglect to apply to private colleges as well, preferably colleges where that student could be offered additional merit-based aid due to their skill set. If the student has good grades, or some other desirable attribute, the student may receive an aid package that makes an expensive private school cheaper to attend than the local community college.

Remember, by good grades we are not necessarily talking straight As. At many colleges, there are scholarships available for students with a B average and combined SAT scores of over 1,000 (or the ACT equivalent). Sometimes even students with C averages and high need get generous aid packages at good, but less selective, private colleges.

If You Have High Need

For most families with an EFC of between $5,000 and $20,000, an out-of-state public university is the most expensive option they could possibly choose. Why? First, students from out-of-state are charged a lot more. Second, much of the financial aid at these schools is earmarked for in-state students. Third, you will most likely not be able to take aid from your own state across state lines. Fourth, if the student is likely to fit into the top half of the entering class, he will probably get a better deal from a private college.

Families with limited means have difficulty imagining that they could get an aid package of $40,000 per year or more, but in fact this is not out of the bounds of reality at all. Choose schools with high endowments where the child will be in the top quarter of the entering class.

Naturally, you can't depend on a huge package from a private college, so again, a financial safety school is a must. For families with high need, the best financial safety school is probably still an in-state public university or community college.

If You Have Moderate Need

A family with an EFC from $20,000 to $35,000 is in a tough position. This is a lot of money to have to come up with every year, perhaps more than you feel you can afford.

A family with moderate need might want to choose two financial safety schools, consisting of either in-state or out-of-state public universities. It may seem like there's voodoo at play, but depending on your circumstances, either choice may actually cost you less than your EFC.

Financial planning is particularly vital to moderate-need families, and strategizing can make a much bigger difference in the size of your aid package than you probably think, and may make it possible for your child to attend a private college. For private colleges, you should again be looking at several schools where the student will be considered desirable and stands a good chance of getting institutional grants and scholarships.

When a college meets a higher percentage of need with grant or scholarship aid versus loans, based on a student's competitiveness, this is called "Preferential packaging." Preferential packaging is particularly important to moderate-need families, as is the practice of applying to a wide variety of schools. By applying to more schools, you increase the likelihood that at least one of the schools will give you a good package. You can then either accept the offer or use it to try to get a better deal at another college.

If You Have Low Need

A family with an EFC of between $35,000 and $55,000 (or more) must decide how much it is willing to pay for what kind of education, and how much debt it is willing to take on. If you are willing to go into debt, then your financial safety school becomes merely a regular safety school.

Even families with anticipated low need should apply for aid. For one thing, with the cost of college being what it is, you may still qualify for some. You also have to look ahead four years. Perhaps your situation will change; for example, you might have only one child in college now, but next year you might have two. Even though any aid this year will not be based on what may happen next year, it will be helpful to your cause next year to have applied this year, even if you do not qualify.

Finally, with their high sticker prices, some private colleges are having trouble filling their classrooms. The FAOs at many of these schools seem to be more and more willing to provide more aid in order to enroll more students. As a result, a family's final family contribution may end up being several thousand dollars less than the need analysis indicated.

The Public Ivies

Over the past few years, the cost of some of the best public universities has risen sky high, to the point at which an out-of-state resident can pay more to attend a public university than a private college. Nevertheless, some of the "public ivies" remain bargains for in-state students, and provide a first-class education at an undervalued price tag. Here are just a few examples of good deals for in-state residents:

	In-state tuition	Out-of-state tuition
Georgia Tech	$10,008	$30,604
SUNY Binghamton	$6,670	$21,550
University of California—Berkeley	$11,220	$37,902
The University of North Carolina at Chapel Hill	$6,881	$32,602
University of Michigan—Ann Arbor	$15,433	$48,814
The University of Texas at Austin	$10,398	$36,744
University of Virginia	$13,412	$44,241
University of Wisconsin—Madison	$9,273	$33,523

*Data reported to The Princeton Review in Spring 2018. Get the most up-to-date information anytime at PrincetonReview.com/College-Search

Financial Aid and Applying Early

Many colleges allow applicants to submit their materials for an early deadline (sometime in the fall) that come before the regular deadline (usually sometime in January or February.)

Let's dig into the terminology.

- Early Decision: Some colleges allow students to apply early and find out early whether or not they have been accepted. You are allowed to apply early decision to only one school, because your application binds both you and the school. Early decision applicants will also need to apply early for aid; be sure to consult the college's admissions literature for early decision financial aid filing requirements. Provided that you meet your deadlines, you should receive an aid package in the same envelope with your acceptance letter. If you are admitted under Early Decision, and if your financial aid package is sufficient to enable your attendance, you are required to withdraw other applications and post a deposit to your ED school (more on this below).

- Early Action: This is an admissions option in which you are notified early of your acceptance but are not bound to attend the school. You have until the normal deadline in May to decide whether to attend. The financial aid package, however, may not arrive in your mailbox until April, unless you submit the FAFSA and/or the CSS Profile at the same time you submit your Early Action application.

- Early Notification: Offered by many colleges that use rolling admissions, this is when the admissions committee mails out acceptance letters as it makes its decisions. Generally, you still have until the normal deadline to let the colleges know if you are accepting their offer. You apply for aid as if you were a regular applicant, and financial aid packages arrive with acceptances or they may come later.

What Are the Financial Aid Implications of These Programs?

When making the decision to apply early, don't forget the financial aid implications of early decision programs.

- Early Decision: For a high-need or moderate-need family, early decision is a big gamble, removes your ability to compare aid packages because you will be admitted with an aid award from your ED school before hearing from other schools to which you have applied. If you want to compare aid packages to take "the best deal" then perhaps Early Decision is not for you, even though in many cases, admission is less competitive in ED. If you are offered insufficient aid, however, you should appeal for more. In today's competitive market, colleges hate to lose ED students and will typically do all they can to retain the student. If after appealing for more aid, the result is still not sufficient to make attendance possible, all colleges will excuse you from your ED commitment and will not require you to withdraw applications from the other schools to which you have applied.

> **TIP** ▶ **Keep Filling Out Applications While You Wait**
>
> We recommend that any student who applies to one school early decision should completely fill out applications to several other schools while waiting to hear. If the student is rejected or deferred by the early decision school—or if the aid package is not enough—then you will have other college options available to you.

- Early action: Even if student s are accepted early action, they should probably still apply to several schools in order to compare financial aid offers and, if necessary, to use a better offer from one school to appeal for more assistance at another.

- Early notification: The only financial aid implications of early notification occur if you are being squeezed. If a college is putting pressure on you to accept an offer of admission before you have heard from other schools, simply tell them that you have until May 1 to reply and that you need to wait to hear from other schools. It is a violation of accepted good practice in admissions to ask for a deposit from a non-ED student before May 1.

Don't Worry About Getting Tied Down Early (Action or Notification, at Least)

An early action or early notification acceptance (unlike a "restrictive early decision" acceptance) does not bind the student to go to that school. The college is just letting you know early on that you have a spot if you want it. Your child has just been accepted by her first-choice school, which is great news, but you may not receive an aid package for several months. To avoid this, apply for financial aid at the same time that you apply for admission. Then you will have all of the information you need to make a wise financial decision once you hear from the other colleges to which you have applied.

Getting Creative With Your College List

We'll go into this more in-depth in Step 8, but your main takeaway from this chapter should be that it's important to remember you can start thinking of ways to minimize your college tuition bill before the application process even begins!

> **TIP** Try looking into schools with "cooperative education" programs.
>
> Over 900 colleges allow students to combine college education with a job. It can take longer to complete a degree this way, but graduates generally owe less in student loans and have a better chance of getting hired.

Establishing Residency Within a State

Establishing residency in another state is probably worthwhile only if the school you want to attend is a public university with lower in-state rates. The difference between in-state and out- of-state rates can be more than $25,000. It is true that in-state residents also may qualify for additional state grant aid available for students who attend public or private colleges, but this will generally be less than $4,000 a year—sometimes a lot less.

Whether you will be able to pull this off at all is another story. Each state has its own residency requirements and, within those requirements, different rules that govern your eligibility for state grants and your eligibility for in-state tuition rates at a public university. These days, the requirements are usually very tough and they are getting tougher. To find out about residency requirements for a school in a particular state, consult the financial aid office at that school.

Don't Let the Price Tag Get You Just Yet

The rub of the application process is that you find out the admission decision and the financial aid award, and financial-wise, almost simultaneously. You'll likely have your EFC in hand by the time applications are going in, but you still won't know exactly what that means until you have the award letters in hand, especially given the available financial aid. Talk with your child realistically and don't buckshot the applications process (there are fees, after all), but don't allow the prospect of price to affect the application process any more than it needs to.

STEP FOUR

Apply for Financial Aid
NO MATTER What

As we said in the Introduction, people are surprised at how much money you have to make in order NOT to qualify for aid. If your butler is currently reading this aloud to you during your daily massage, you're probably all set in terms of tuition...but you should still apply for financial aid. You never know what formulas are at play or how an institution's private funds may be meted out.

In fact, some merit-based aid can only be awarded if the applicant has submitted financial aid application forms. So apply for financial aid no matter your circumstances. Determine early on which forms you must file, and when they are due.

The Standardized Forms

We already covered the basic process for applying for aid in Step 1, but as a refresher, here's a list of the forms:

- Free Application for Federal Student Aid (FAFSA)

- CSS Profile

- Supplemental forms

TIP When applying to several schools you should keep in mind that you are only allowed to file one FAFSA form per student per year. The form will have a space where the student can list the schools they'll be applying to (and more can be added later on).

After you click Submit on your form or forms, the data is sent to a processing service, which then sends out reports to you and to the colleges you designate. If you recall from Step 1, you and your colleges will receive a report called the Student Aid Report (or SAR) based on your FAFSA data. If you also file the CSS Profile, you will receive an Acknowledgment/Data Confirmation Report from the College Board which lists the schools to which your CSS Profile was sent and summarizes the data submitted.

1. Figure Out Which Form(s) to Fill Out

As you narrow down your list of colleges, you've got the unenviable task of finding out which financial aid forms are required by which schools. NOTE: The FAFSA will be required by all colleges for federal grants and student and parent loans.

The very best form requirement and deadline information comes from the school's own financial aid office website. Many college guides, including The Princeton Review's' own *The Complete Book of Colleges*, publish this information, but you should always double-check with each of the colleges on your list.

Start with the FAFSA

Any prospective U.S. college student who wants to be considered for federal financial aid must complete the Free Application for Federal Student Aid. The Department of Education offers three options:

1.   The FAFSA on the Web (also known as the FOTW)

2.   The paper FAFSA

3.   The Downloadable PDF FAFSA—Instead of using the regular paper version of the FAFSA, you can also download, complete, print, and submit a PDF version.

We highly recommend going the FAFSA on the Web route. While this choice will not affect how the processor calculates your EFC under the federal formula, there are a number of advantages to filing the FOTW form:

Advantage #1: You can list up to ten schools to receive your data (compared to only four with the paper or PDF version of the form). After you receive your SAR, you can add even more schools!

Advantage #2: You don't need to worry about the post office losing your form or delivering it late.

Advantage #3: The online FAFSA form has an interactive data retrieval tool that takes you to an IRS website that allows you to transfer some information from that year's completed tax return directly onto the FAFSA.

Advantage #4: Your FAFSA data will be processed faster.

Advantage #5: The skip logic built into the online form helps you to avoid providing inconsistent data.

Advantage #6: You don't have to worry that some responses on the paper or PDF FAFSA will be subject to a FAFSA "fat finger" error, resulting in a typo.

TIP **Where to Find the FAFSA**

Details on how to complete the FOTW or how to download the PDF version are available on the Department of Education's FAFSA web page (www.fafsa.ed.gov).

You can obtain a copy of the paper FAFSA form by calling 1 800 4-FED-AID (1-800 433-3243). Be sure to specify which year's form you need.

Do Any of Your Colleges Require the CSS Profile?

If you are applying to private colleges (as well as a few state schools) you may also have to complete the College Board's CSS Profile.

Many private colleges and a handful of state schools will require completion of the oft-mentioned CSS Profile form in addition to the FAFSA for anyone who wishes to be considered for institutional as well as federal aid—and you're not one to turn down free money. We'll go into the major differences between completing the FAFSA and CSS Profile form at the end of this chapter.

Fees and Timing: Unlike the FAFSA, the CSS Profile form can only be obtained by first creating an online account at CollegeBoard.org. There is a $25 CSS Profile application fee and a $16 processing fee per school (the first one is included in the application fee), so you'll want to make sure that your child is certain or relatively certain that they'll be applying to a college before you submit. Be sure to carefully review each college's financial aid requirements regarding CSS Profile information (if at all). Certain users may be eligible for a fee waiver for up to the first eight colleges/programs. There are also some private scholarship programs that require the CSS Profile.

TIP You Can Add More Schools to Your CSS Profile Later

Once you've submitted your CSS Profile, additional schools can be added at a later time, subject to the same $16 processing fee. You will be asked any additional supplemental questions that are required by the added school(s) but have not been previously asked.

Do Any of Your Colleges Require Their Own Aid Forms?

In case your desk and mind aren't cluttered enough, some schools have their own aid applications as well. These schools require you to fill out their supplemental financial aid forms in addition to the FAFSA and CSS Profile. For example, any incoming first-year students applying for financial aid at the University of Pennsylvania must complete the Penn Financial Aid Supplement in addition to the forms listed above.

Supplemental forms are very important, so carefully check through the admissions applications of the schools to which your child is applying to see if any supplemental aid forms are required. Unlike the FAFSA and CSS Profile, supplemental forms must be sent directly to the individual colleges.

You'll begin to notice that many of the questions on these forms are identical, and are meant to drill down further into questions already asked on the FAFSA and/or the CSS Profile form, or to try and sniff out inconsistencies among your responses. Individual schools may also ask a few questions that seem odd for a form, but don't worry. Financial aid officers are just trying to find recipients for restricted awards donated by alumni that the aid office would prefer to award before they begin to dole out their unrestricted funds.

TIP   **Make Sure It's the Right Version of the Form**

Double check that you are using the most up-to-date version of the form. Don't laugh: It's very easy to use last year's form because of the overlap in processing, and you've probably got a few other things on your mind, anyway.

---

2. Know Your Deadlines

Missing a financial aid deadline is worse than forgetting your significant other's birthday. Your significant other will likely give you another chance. Colleges may not.

Applicants and returning students can file the FAFSA and the CSS Profile as early as October 1 every year. Keep in mind that schools process their financial aid candidates in batches. Aid applications are collected in a pile up until the "Priority Filing Deadline," which is set by each school, and then assessed in one batch. If you send in your application way ahead of the deadline, you will not necessarily be better off than someone who just squeezes by, except in so far as you are more likely to receive a response WITH your letter of admission rather than way later. However, if your application arrives a day late, it could sit unopened in the late application pile until the entire first batch has been given aid. Then, if there is anything left in their coffers, the financial aid officers assess the second batch on a rolling basis.

Types of Deadlines

Remember, that there are three types of financial aid deadlines:

- Mailed By: Application must be mailed (and postmarked) by a particular date.

- Received By: Application must be received and "date stamped" by the need analysis company by a particular date.

- Processed By: Your standardized application must be processed and the results made available to the school, private scholarship program, or state agency by a certain date.

Carefully check the language for each school to make sure you're logging the right deadline in your tracker.

You should also realize that the school's deadline for the FAFSA and the CSS Profile (if required by the school) may be different. However, because the filing periods for both forms begins on October 1 and because consistency between forms is important, it is generally a good idea to submit both the FAFSA and CSS Profile at the same time. Keep in mind that while the information relating to the prior-prior year income will involve a time period that has long since ended, (two tax years prior th the year of enrollment), the asset information and other demographic details of your situation is current to the date you submit the form.

To make matters more confusing, the school's deadlines for their own aid forms (supplemental forms) may be different from the school's deadlines for the FAFSA and/or the CSS Profile! Which leads us to...

How to Keep Track of Deadlines

There are so many different deadlines to remember during the process of applying for college admission and financial aid that the only way to keep everything straight is to write it all down in one place. We suggest that you use the handy checklist that appears on page 73.

In summary, here are the deadlines you should be tracking for each college you plan to apply to:

1. School deadline for the FAFSA (mailed by/received by/or processed by)

2. School deadline for the CSS Profile (mailed by/received by/or processed by)

3. School deadline for supplemental forms

4. School deadlines for scholarship applications, if any

5. School deadline for application for admission

When's the Best Time to Submit Aid Forms?

This is one of those questions to which you'd most like a firm answer, but unfortunately that answer is entirely dependent on your situation and the schools you or your child have decided to apply to.

While conventional wisdom holds that one should always file "as soon as possible after X", the reality is that you should file at the appropriate time when your snapshot will show the greatest need for aid.

1. If you are applying for aid at one of the few schools that still awards financial aid on a first come, first served (FCFS) basis instead of a prior ity filing date, then you should file the 2019–2020 aid forms as soon as possible after October 1st.

2. If you reside in one of the states that awards state aid on an FCFS basis until funds run out (refer back to the Intro for a list), then you also want to file the FAFSA and other required forms ASAP after October 1st. More on State Aid in Step 5.

3. If neither of the first two situations apply to you, the earliest school's priority deadline becomes your overall final deadline, and you should file the form at the point between October 1st and this date during a time when your family contribution is likely to be the lowest number.

TIP ▸ **No U.S. Tax Return?**

If you are not required to file a U.S. tax return, it's no worry: the financial aid application process and forms are designed to also accommodate those who don't file a tax return (or those who are only required to file a foreign tax return).

---

3. Round up the Paperwork Required to Complete the Forms

Since the FAFSA and CSS Profile will use information from the "prior-prior year" (PPY, or in layman's terms, two tax returns prior to the year of enrollment), you'll luckily already have your tax documents complete, but this isn't going to be a simple copying job. A ten-year-old child can fill out the form, but HOW you fill it out will determine your aid package, so you'll want to make sure you've got all of the tools in your belt.

As you will soon find out, the questions involving PPY income will still only encompass only part of the data required to submit. You should begin gathering all this information together in the weeks before you plan to complete and submit the aid forms.

Paperwork Checklist

For the FAFSA, you will need:

- Completed federal tax return for the base income year (two calendar years before the year you or your student will enter college)

- W-2 forms for the base income year

- Records of any untaxed income for the base income year, if applicable. Examples include social security payments received, welfare payments, tax-exempt interest income, etc.

- Bank statements for the base income year for verification of interest income; current bank statements for current assets

- Brokerage statements for the base income year and the current year, if applicable

- Mortgage statements for properties other than the primary residence for the base income year and the current year, if applicable

- Student's social security number (and driver's license number if the student has one)

- If you are an owner of a business, the business's financial statements or corporate tax return for the base income year

- Other investment statements and records (including any farm you own, but don't live on and operate) for the base income year

- Records of child support paid or received during the base income year

For the CSS Profile, in addition to the 10 items above, you will also need:

- Records of medical and dental expenses paid during the base income year

- Records of any post-secondary tuition paid or that will be paid during the academic year before the year which you are applying for aid

- Records of any educational loan payments made or to be made during the two calendar years prior to the year for which you are applying for aid

- Mortgage statements for your primary residence for the base and current income year, if applicable

- Financial aid awarded to any member of your household, if applicable, for the academic year before the year which you are applying for aid.

TIP Use Whole Dollar Amounts

Regardless of the way you file a form, use whole dollars—no cents or decimals. Also, when writing down the numeric equivalent of a single-digit date, the MMDDYYYY format is usually requested. Thus, January 5, 1995 would look like this: 01051995.

---

4. Do a Dry Run of the Forms

Now is not the time to get sloppy or have to locate the Wite-Out. You should do a practice run of the forms before you touch the hard copy or hit submit on the electronic version. If you're completing a paper FAFSA, make a photocopy first and work off of that before transferring the final numbers over to the hard copy. Only the original form or the PDF version of the FAFSA will be accepted by the FAFSA processor.

If you're filing electronically, you should fill out a worksheet copy of the form before you start inputting your responses online. For the FAFSA you could either print out the worksheet version of the form online or work off a paper version of the form. For the CSS Profile you can print out the worksheet copy provided by the processor.

Marrying the FAFSA with the CSS Profile

The majority of students apply to schools that only require the FAFSA. However, for those students who must also complete the CSS Profile: it would be best if possible to complete the CSS Profile before the FAFSA, as long as you do not risk missing any FAFSA deadline for any other non-CSS Profile schools or state aid programs that may require earlier submission than your earliest CSS Profile school's aid deadlines.

This is because the FAFSA is a cakewalk compared to the CSS Profile, which requires significantly more detailed information than the federal form. Or, as one senior administrator at the College Board once said: "FAFSA is to grade point average as CSS Profile is to an academic transcript."

Which Parent(s) Must Report Information on the FAFSA and CSS Profile?

Both the FAFSA and the CSS Profile have similar guidelines as to which of the student's parents' information is required to be reported. Be aware that this determination is made based on the situation on the date the aid form is completed, not the situation during the prior-prior year. You'll eventually go through the various requirements with a fine-tooth comb, but the gist is:

- If the biological and/or adoptive parents of the student are living together, then information from both parents must be reported regardless of their marital status and regardless of their genders.

- If the biological and/or adoptive parents of the student are living apart (i.e.: divorced, separated, or never married), then only the parent with whom the student spent the most time in the 12-month period prior to completing the FAFSA should report parental information on both forms and will be known as the "custodial parent". If that amount of time is exactly equal, then the parent who provided the greater amount of support during the past 12 months will be the criteria used, regardless of which parent claims the student on their taxes, has custody, and/or which parent is legally responsible to pay for college.

- If a divorced or widowed parent is remarried (or the student's parents were never married, but now the biological or adoptive parent is married to someone other than the student's other parent), then the information of the custodial parent and custodial step-parent must be reported.

- If one of the student's biological or adopted parents is deceased and the surviving parent is not married, then only the surviving parent's information is reported.

How do I get a FSA ID?

If you are filling out the FAFSA online, you'll be invited to enter the student's FSA ID. If you don't have one, you can start by entering the student information instead—but it actually makes sense to get an FSA ID before you start filling out the FAFSA.

Now, the FSA ID has been causing confusion since it was introduced, so don't worry if you encounter some mix-ups. The FSA ID has several useful functions, all of which make it worth the trouble:

- It can serve as a signature when you submit your FAFSA.

- It permits you to access your processed FAFSA data at a later date, and if necessary revise or correct it.

- It permits you to apply for federal education loans online.

- It allows you to access your federal education loan history via the National Student Loan Data System (NSLDS).

- It allows you to complete the Agreement to Serve (ATS) for the federal TEACH grant program.

Despite all of the benefits, what the FSA ID does NOT do is serve as a "password" for your FOTW application prior to submission. This is the function of the "Save Key", which you'll create early on. If you don't start and submit the FAFSA in one session (and no one really does), you'll need this "Save Key" to go back online and access your previously-saved FOTW data.

TIP ▸ **Both the Student and the Parent Create Their Own FSA IDs**

Because the FAFSA of a dependent student must be signed by both the student and one parent/step-parent whose information is reported on the FAFSA, both the student and the parent/step-parent must create their own FSA ID user name and password combination.

Tips for Actually Filling Out the Forms

You're going to spend plenty of time going through the forms line by line so we won't get granular, but we will offer some tips to keep in mind throughout. If you want line-by-line instructions, check out our comprehensive financial aid guide, *Paying for College*.

1.   "You" refers to the student. Roll your eyes if you must, but you'd be surprised how often pronouns get crossed, particularly if the parent is the one filling out the need analysis forms in their entirety. It may seem like a no-brainer when filling out a name, but when the form asks for marital status, it's not as obvious. Any section specifically meant for parental information will be clearly marked.

2.   If you have two children applying for aid, you must fill out two separate forms. Even though the information will be mostly the same or the children are planning to attend the same college.

3.   It doesn't hurt to be considered for work-study. You want the colleges to come up with their best offer before you start to commit yourself. If you indicate you are interested in work- study, you can always change your mind later. This question has no effect on grant or scholarship eligibility.

4.   Make sure your child qualifies as an independent student before he or she files as one. It used to be that claiming the student was an independent was a popular financial aid loophole that many parents took advantage of; however, colleges and the government have since cracked down and the rules get more stringent every year. If you're going the independent route, be prepared to provide extensive documentation to the financial aid office. Generally, students under the age of 24 cannot claim independence unless they are a ward of the court or there is some other unusual circumstance.

5.   You may be able to cut out some steps using the IRS Data Retrieval Tool. If you are filing the FOTW (web version) and the student and/or parent(s) have already filed the prior-prior year's taxes, then you be able to use the "IRS Data Retrieval Tool" (or DRT) to have your income tax data automatically transferred from the IRS database onto the form. This also reduces the chances your application will be subject to additional scrutiny through a federal financial aid process known as "Verification."

6.   Check and see if you meet the criteria for the Simplified Needs Test or the Automatic Zero-EFC. Many parents without a simple tax situation will probably be filing their taxes using the 1040 form, but if the parents can file the 1040A or the 1040EZ form (or are not required to file any tax return), it may be advantageous to see if you qualify for the Simplified Needs Test (which excludes all assets from the federal formula) or the Automatic Zero-EFC.

7.   Double check the school codes you are listing on the forms. Whether you're filing on paper or online, take great care in making sure that the codes for the schools that will receive the reports are correct. If you are applying to a particular branch or division of a university, be sure to use the correct code for that branch or division.

8.   List the schools with the earliest FAFSA deadlines first. The paper and the FOTW FAFSAs allow you to list four and ten schools, respectively. If you are submitting to more than the allotted number of schools, you should first list those schools with the earliest FAFSA deadlines. If you are applying to any schools in your home state, we recommend that you list at least one of them first on the FAFSA. After your FAFSA has been processed, you can always have the data sent to the colleges you did not list on the FAFSA.

9.   If you aren't sure about housing, put "on-campus" to be safe. The FAFSA requires that you list a housing code for each school you specify, so if you're unsure of the student's living situation put "on-campus", since the cost of attendance will be higher and you will qualify for more aid as a result.)

Differences Between the CSS Profile and the FAFSA

If you are required to fill out the CSS Profile, know that many of the questions on the form will correspond exactly to the questions on the FAFSA, but some similarly worded questions may require a different response. You'll be reading through thoroughly as you go, but before you start, here is a very dry briefing on the important differences between the CSS Profile and the FAFSA.

- On the CSS Profile, real estate (other than your primary residence) should not be included as an "Investment", and will be listed in a separate category: "Other real estate."

- Regarding certain assets, the CSS Profile requires you to list "What is it worth today" (value) and "What is owed on it" (debt) separately. The College Board will then do the subtraction for you to determine your net assets.

- Even if you can skip the asset questions on the online FAFSA, you must answer all the asset questions on the CSS Profile.

- Unlike the FAFSA, which only asks for financial information of the custodial parent, the CSS Profile process provides schools the opportunity to request information from the non-custodial parent (and if applicable, the step-parent residing with the non-custodial parent) when the student's biological or adoptive parents are no longer living together. However, the non-custodial parent's information will go on a separate application.

- In most cases, students completing the FAFSA who meet the federal definition of "independent" do not need to provide parental financial information on the FAFSA.

5. You're Done! Sit Back and Wait for Your SAR

After you've checked, photocopied, and submitted, it's time to relax. Your only job now is to await your Student Aid Report.

If you filed a paper version of the FAFSA and did not provide an e-mail address, the government will send you your SAR a few weeks after you submit your FAFSA to the processor. (You can also retrieve the SAR online at fafsa.ed.gov provided you have a verified FSA ID for the student.) If you filed the FAFSA and provided a student e-mail address on either the paper or online version, you will need to retrieve your SAR electronically, as no paper SAR will be mailed to the student. No matter which method you used, check and make sure the information on the SAR agrees with the information you entered on the FAFSA.

 TIP In case you run into any trouble along the way, the DOE has a comprehensive support system in place to provide help with the FAFSA submission process:

Federal Student Aid Information Center: 1-800-4FED-AID (Note. The contact center can discuss FSA ID issues only with the owner of the FSA ID)

After You Submit: What Happens Next?

First, you'll receive your Student Aid Report. The SAR will tell you:

- If you qualify for a Pell Grant

- Your Expected Family Contribution (EFC)

Somehow, no matter how prepared you are, seeing the federal EFC in print is always a shock. Remember that your actual family contribution toward college expenses could be lower or higher than the EFC printed on the SAR. Schools that asked you to fill out the CSS Profile form will most likely be using the institutional methodology to determine the family contribution. and usually that EFC is higher than what is printed on the SAR, especially for families with home equity. Colleges have some latitude to change the Federal EFC in either direction, but they must follow strict guidelines when doing so, as it will impact federal aid eligibility. Read more about appealing your awards from colleges in Step 6.

The Verification Process

Verification is the financial aid version of an audit, though the process is generally more benign! The Federal processor will determine who must be selected for verification, but schools can also add individual students.

- If you estimated your tax information, you are more likely to be verified.

- The lower your EFC, the more likely you are to be verified.

- If you filled out the paper version of the FAFSA, you're more likely to be verified.

- If you say you've already completed your taxes, but don't use the IRS data retrieval tool (automatically pre-populating the FAFSA form from IRS records)—you are more likely to be selected for verification.

While the IRS audits a small percentage of taxpayers, financial aid verification is relatively common place. At some schools, 100 percent of the applicants are verified. The bottom line is that if you receive a notice of verification, there is no need to worry. It is all routine.

What happens if you need to revise your information?

If the numbers on the Student Aid Report are different from the numbers you sent in, you will probably want to revise them immediately. The SAR gives you instructions on how to correct errors made either by the process or by you. You will want to revise immediately if you receive any notice stating that your FAFSA could not be processed, if there are comments on the SAR that there were problems with e-processing, or if you need to change the list of schools.

Supplying Completed Tax Returns

Some colleges will not give a financial aid package until they've seen your taxes for the first base income year. Others will give you a "tentative" package, subject to change when they see the actual tax return. Find out from colleges that you are interested in whether they really do want to see your tax return. We recommend that you do not send a return unless it is required.

Find and Apply for Grants and Scholarships

At this point it should come as no surprise that the next item on your financial aid To-Do List is "apply for more things," but the good news is those "things" can result in free money! Whether you've already submitted your FAFSA and/or CSS Profile and are beginning scholarship and grant applications in sequence, you're overlapping the processes, or you've put it entirely in the hands of your child (remember, this is an option!), scholarships and grants are going to seem like a treat compared to the need analysis forms.

The Different Types of Grants and Scholarships

You'll remember from Step 1 that grants and scholarships are the best part of the aid package, because they don't require repayment—they're essentially money in your pocket. While you can accept or reject any part of the package you are offered, you're never going to want to say no to grants or scholarships. Let's look at them a little more in-depth.

Grants

Grant money can come from the government, the state, or the institution itself (or any combination therein), but it's free and clear, and almost always tax-free. All federal grants are awarded only to U.S. citizens or eligible noncitizens. Grants can come in different forms:

- **The Federal Pell Grant:** The Pell is primarily for low-income families. You automatically apply for the Pell Grant when you fill out the FAFSA. The size of the award is decided by the federal government and cannot be adjusted by the colleges. If you qualify, you will receive up to $6,095 per year, based on need.

- **The Federal Supplemental Educational Opportunity Grant (or SEOG):** This is a federal grant that is administered by the colleges themselves. Each year, the schools get a lump sum that they are allowed to dispense to the neediest students at their own discretion. The size of the award runs from $100 to $4,000 per year per student.

- **Grants from the Schools Themselves:** Since this money comes out of the college's coffers, these grants are in effect discounts off the college's sticker price. As this is not taxpayer money, there are no rules about how it must be dispensed. The school can dispense it based on whatever logic it chooses; some schools say they award money solely based on need, but many schools also give out merit-based awards. There is no limit on the size of a grant from an individual school—it could range from a few hundred dollars to a full-ride scholarship. Each school, however, will have its own policies regarding minimum and maximum grant values.

- **State Grants:** If a student is attending college in his state of legal residence, or in a state that has a reciprocal agreement with their state of legal residence (more on that in a bit), then they may also qualify for a state grant. These grants are based on need, as well as on the cost of tuition at a particular school, and are administered by the states themselves.

- **The Teacher Education Assistance for College and Higher Education (TEACH) Grant Program:** This federal grant program provides grants of up to $4,000 per year to students who intend to teach full-time in a high need field in a private elementary or secondary school that serves students from low-income families. To qualify, students must attend a participating school and meet certain academic requirements.

Scholarships

Scholarships are also free money, but can be conditional—i.e. the student must maintain a certain GPA or continue playing a sport for the college. Contrary to popular belief, most scholarship dollars are usually awarded by the schools themselves, and the amount of money available from outside scholarships is actually quite small. Unlike grants, the breakdown is pretty binary:

- **Scholarships from the School:** Some schools use the words grants and scholarships interchangeably, and award them similarly—in other words, based on need. Other schools give merit-based scholarships based on either academic, athletic, or artistic talent. Some schools give scholarships based on a combination of the two. As far as you're concerned, the only thing that matters is whether the scholarship is used to meet need or whether it may be used to reduce your family contribution. (NOTE: Institutional scholarships cannot be used to reduce the federal EFC if there is any federal grant, loan or work-study funds in the financial aid package along with the institutional scholarship)

- **Outside Scholarships:** If you have won a scholarship from a source not affiliated with the college (such as a local community organization), you are required to tell the colleges about it—often the scholarship donor will even notify the colleges you applied to directly. In some cases, the schools will use the outside scholarship to reduce the amount of grant money they were going to give you; in other cases, colleges might reduce your need to borrow or work—we'll cover this more at the end of the chapter. In other words, winning a scholarship does not mean you will pay less money for college; your family contribution often stays exactly the same, and it has to under federal regulations if there is federal money awarded in your aid package..

 A Word of Caution

You should never pay money to investigate scholarships. Scholarship providers don't offer their awards to students who pay to find them; they offer them to all students. Steer clear of scholarship search websites that ask you to pay a fee.

State Aid

All fifty states have need-based financial aid programs for their residents, and more than 25 states now have merit-based awards as well. We've moved past the simplicity of in- versus out-of-state tuition rates here: now we're talking about the need-based and merit-based grants and loans to qualifying students who attend public or private colleges and universities within their own state. While some states are richer than others, the amount of money available for state aid is substantial. For the latest information on the availability of aid in your state, contact the appropriate state agency.

Federal and State Aid are Calculated Differently

Even if you don't quality for federal aid, you may quality for state aid. The aid formulas differ both between states and the federal government. Federal aid is based on your adjusted gross income (AGI) along with your assets, but in some states, aid is based solely on your taxable income (the AGI minus deductions) without reference to your assets. If you miss out on federal aid because you've wisely invested money, you may be able to qualify for state money anyway. That means that in some states, you can own a house, boat, houseboat, and a healthy portfolio, and—as long as your taxable income is within state parameters—still qualify for thousands of dollars in aid.

Tuition Reciprocity Agreements

To qualify for this aid a student usually must be going to a public university or private college within their state of legal residence, but a few states have reciprocal agreements with specific other states that allow you to take aid with you to another state. Be sure to check with your specific state for an up-to-date list of reciprocity agreements, but some of the larger programs for member institutions include:

- Midwest Student Exchange: Public institutions agree to charge qualifying non-resident students no more than 150 percent of the in-state resident tuition rate for specific programs; private institutions offer a 10 percent reduction on their tuition rates. Participating states are Illinois, Indiana, Kansas, Michigan, Minnesota, Missouri, Nebraska, North Dakota, Ohio, or Wisconsin.

- Academic Common Market: This Southern Regional Education Board program provides tuition discounts for more than 1900 qualifying undergraduate and graduate programs in the member states of Alabama, Arkansas, Delaware, Florida, Georgia, Kentucky, Louisiana, Maryland, Mississippi, Oklahoma, South Carolina, Tennessee, Texas, Virginia, and West Virginia.

- New England Regional Student Program: The Tuition Break program lets New England residents get a discount at out-of-state New England public colleges and universities when they enroll in an approved major that is not offered by public colleges and universities in their home state. New England residents are defined as being from Connecticut, Maine, Massachusetts, New Hampshire, Rhode Island, and Vermont.

- Western Undergraduate Exchange: This public university-only reciprocity agreement allows residents of member states to enroll in more than 150 participating two- and four-year public institutions at 150 percent of the in-state tuition. Member states include Alaska, Arizona, California, Colorado, Hawaii, Idaho, Montana, New Mexico, Nevada, North Dakota, Oregon, South Dakota, Utah, Washington, and Wyoming.

How to Apply for State Aid

Some states use the data you supply on the federal FAFSA form to award their aid. Other states require you fill out a supplemental aid form which will be processed directly by that state's higher education agency. Students, check with your high school counselor, who can direct you to the correct forms.

If your family is eligible for state financial aid, your state grant will appear as part of the aid packages you receive from the colleges sometime before April 15. Take note: unless your state has reciprocal agreements, the state money will appear only in the aid packages from colleges in your own state. So if you are eligible for state aid as a resident of Virginia, you can't apply it to a University of California aid package.

Families considering multiple schools within their own state might notice that state award amounts at each of the schools may differ. This is because aid is based not just on need, but also on the size of tuition at different schools. A more expensive school will often trigger a larger grant. This is particularly true when comparing state grant awards at public versus private institutions. Students at private colleges within a state will typically see higher state grants awards due to the higher tuition charged.

> **TIP** Comparing State Aid Packages
>
> If you applied to two comparably priced schools within your own state and the aid packages differ greatly, then something is amiss— students should be getting approximately the same amount of state aid at similarly priced schools.

How to Find Scholarships

Perhaps the most "findable" of all scholarships are those administered by the colleges themselves. Most schools will host a scholarship page on their website that lists the scholarships available to current and incoming students and the qualifications for each. The colleges know they have this money available, and it will go to the candidates who meet the requirements, based on the information available on the financial aid forms and the student application itself. Some institutional scholarships require separate scholarship applications, so do your research! It is in the colleges' best interest to award these "restricted" scholarships first since this frees up unrestricted funds for other students. Every year, colleges award virtually all the scholarship money they have at their disposal. What may not go awarded is outside scholarships.

Opinions are divided about outside scholarships. The companies that sell scholarship databases say there are thousands of unclaimed scholarships just waiting to be found, while critics say that very few scholarships actually go unclaimed each year, and the database search companies are providing lists that one can get from government agencies, the local library, or the internet for free.

We've encountered parents who have had terrible experiences with the scholarship search companies, and others who swear by them—it's going to be up to you to make the call. Just keep in mind that this type of aid accounts for less than 5 percent of the financial aid in the United States (which is still a hefty chunk of change).

6 Resources for Finding College Scholarships

1. **Your high school counselor's office**
   The office often maintains a database or binder of scholarships for students to browse during application season. Think of your guidance as your advance scholarship scout.

2. **The college's own financial aid office and website**
   This is going to be your primary resource in finding awards. Though many schools consider the admissions application to also be a scholarship application, there are still sometimes lists of outside scholarships that must be applied for separately, or require additional materials.

3. **Vetted scholarship search tools**
   Paid scholarship search companies can be hit-or-miss, but there are a few free search tools (such as the U.S. Department of Labor's scholarship finder, or Sallie Mae's) that can be trusted, and will likely find most of the same scholarships with no risk.

4. **Local library bulletin boards or career centers**
   Local organizations often post scholarships in public domains. The money may not be huge, but every little bit counts.

5. **Parent(s)' employers**
   Employers (particularly larger corporations) often have scholarships specifically for the children of employees. This is a relatively smaller competitive pool that often has a lot of money to hand out.

6. **Local community organizations (via newspapers, community and cultural centers)**
   Many local civic and religious groups, professional organizations and unions, and small businesses give out small scholarships to area students. If these weren't found on bulletin boards somewhere, they'll often be included in the newspaper or local congregational buildings.

Scholarships for Scores

Some scholarship awards come directly as a result of high standardized test scores. The most well-known is available to every PSAT-taking junior in the country.

National Merit Scholarships: Do you know the PSAT's full name? It's the National Merit Scholarship Qualifying Test (hereafter referred to as PSAT/NMSQT). The National Merit Scholarship Corporation (NMSC) gives out about 1,800 non-renewable scholarships and 2,800 renewable college-sponsored scholarships to students who score extremely well on the PSAT/NMSQT, which acts as the qualifier for entry into a particular year's "competition." Did we mention how important test prep is? In 2017, out of 1.6 million juniors who took the PSAT/NMSQT some 7,500 finalists received National Merit Scholarship awards.

At schools where all financial aid is need-based, a National Merit finalist will not necessarily get one penny of institutional aid unless "need" is demonstrated. Other schools, however, may give National Merit finalists a sponsored scholarship that could range up to a four-year full scholarship.

Guaranteed Scholarships: A number of colleges and universities offer "guaranteed" scholarships based on SAT and/or ACT scores as well as GPA or class rank. At some schools you will be considered automatically when you apply for admission; others require a scholarship application by a certain deadline. Another great reason to explore scholarships opportunities early on!

Major National Scholarships

Coca-Cola Scholars Program Scholarship: An achievement-based scholarship recognizing students for their capacity to lead and serve, as well as their commitment to making a significant impact on their schools and communities. One hundred fifty seniors are selected to receive this $20,000 award.

Dell Scholars Program: A flexible award for seniors who have demonstrated financial need and have been offered a Pell Grant. The $20,000 award can be used to cover a range of college costs, and students also receive a laptop and textbook credits.

Gates Scholarship: A highly selective, full scholarship (covering the difference between tuition and the financial aid package) for 300 students that have proven academic excellence, and are Pell-eligible, minority, high school seniors.

Davidson Fellows Scholarship: One of the most prestigious scholarships out there, The Davidson Fellows Scholarship awards $50,000, $25,000 and $10,000 scholarships to extraordinary young people who have completed a significant piece of work in the fields of science, technology, engineering, mathematics, literature, music, and philosophy.

Local Scholarships: While the big money may be in the larger national scholarships that you'll no doubt hear about during your senior year, the more realistic money can be found in local scholarships, which will be less competitive. It'll also be easier to infuse these applications with personalized references and recommendations. Local scholarship award amounts can really cover a range, but remember that every little bit helps. There's no limit to the number of scholarships you can apply to, so apply to every one you're eligible for.

Scholarship Applications

No doubt you're an expert completer of forms at this point, but scholarship applications require a bit of a reset from financial aid forms and college applications. The good news is that some of the applications are simply basic information, and the ones that require an essay will almost always give you a prompt for a topic. A great scholarship application—its essays and short answers—helps the scholarship provider understand the real person behind the application and can be the key to winning the award (assuming you meet the other scholarship criteria).

No Time for Modesty

In many cases, there is no separate application for college-administered scholarships, and students are automatically considered for available scholarships when they apply for admissions. The schools select the recipients with a keen eye toward enticing high-caliber students to attend. That's why it's important for the student to sell themselves in the application. If the student is an accomplished saxophonist, that should come up in essays, recommendations from music teachers, even supplementary materials such as news clippings.

Also, if a student is offered one or more of these merit-based scholarships, it is important to find out if it's a one-time award or renewable based on performance. If renewable, just how good does the student's academic performance have to be in order to get the same award next year?

Mine Your Interests

Even beyond just sports and academic pursuits, your hobbies are a great jumping-off point to look for related scholarships that you can apply for, or to work into application essays for more straightforward scholarships.

Many local awards especially are targeted toward specific groups, interests, or backgrounds, so even if the essay is open-ended, you've already got some direction. If it's a community organization, speak of your work in the community, or your history within it; if it's an organization based on a particular interest, share how you came by knowledge of the subject, and so on. You get the jist.

When to Apply for Scholarships

Unlike the somewhat tricky timing of need analysis forms with respect to the tax season and deadlines, scholarships have a flat out directive: apply early, and apply often. Scholarship deadlines can range from a full year before the student starts college right up through college itself, and there's no downside to getting the application in early.

Additionally, some awards come as a result of the student's performance in college—an example is the Harry S. Truman Scholarship for which students are nominated by their institution based on their achievements in leadership, public service, and academics. Your college financial aid office will keep a catalog of currently available scholarships, which often go overlooked by students during the hustle and bustle of attending school, but it's never too late to pick up free money!

Types of Institutional Scholarships

You may find that supplemental forms ask some odd questions to determine eligibility for specific restricted scholarships and grants. In general, these scholarships are left over from a different era when private citizens funded what today seems like weird scholarships in their own name. The colleges don't really like administering these restricted scholarships and would prefer to hand out money on their own terms, but if you are a direct blood descendant of a World War I veteran, the University of Chicago may have some money for you. If you can prove that one of your ancestors traveled on the Mayflower, Harvard may pad your wallet.

Quirky Scholarships

Scholarships don't have to stay within the lines. A few of the quirkier scholarships out there:

National Potato Council Scholarship: Each year, the NPC awards $10,000 to a graduate-level student conducting research for the benefit of the potato industry.

Doodle 4 Google Scholarship: This fun annual award to a high school student gives at least $5,000 to a winning submission of a doodle based on the theme of "What inspires me?"

Chick Evans Scholarship: This is an annual full tuition and housing scholarship for 260 golf caddies that have a strong caddie record, excellent grades, outstanding character and demonstrated financial need.

Talls Club International Scholarship: This award of $1,000 goes to seniors with a minimum height requirement of 5'10" (for women) and 6'2" (for men.)

That being said, there are some standard categories that colleges have chomped at the bit to fill with capable students for decades:

Academically Gifted: Merit grants based on academic performance in high school are becoming more widespread, and we think this is a trend that will continue as schools try to lure the next generation of great minds. However, most of the money awarded to students with high academic performance is less easy to see, and usually comes in the form of preferential packaging, where colleges meet a higher percentage of need with scholarships or grants versus loans for those top students..

Athletes: Usually the student should sing their qualities in the application; athletes, however, should get in touch with the athletic department directly. When you visit a school, make it a point to meet the coach of the team you want to join—do not assume that a school is not interested in you merely because you have not been approached by a scout during the year. (NOTE: Only colleges in NCAA Division I and II can award scholarships based on athletic ability. In Division III, being a coach-recruited athlete can help with admission, and of course you can't get financial aid from a school unless you get in!)

Legacies: Many colleges will go out of their way for the children of alumni. If the student's parents' circumstances are such that they cannot pay the entire cost of college, they shouldn't hesitate to ask for help; it will even be forthcoming at many schools.

Reporting Your Awards

You should know that when you notify a college that you have won an outside scholarship (and, if you are on financial aid, you are required to tell the school how much you won), at college that meets full need will often deduct that amount from your aid package, (as they are required to do if you also receive federal grants, loans or work-study) and therefore reducing the grants or the loans and work that make up your aid. Thus, if you find and win an outside scholarship, it will often not reduce the bottom line you have to pay now, but it could help to reduce your need to borrow, depending on the individual college's policies. We would suggest that you look on the web or ask the FAO about the school's policy on outside scholarships before you win one.

If you have managed to find and win an outside scholarship, you may want to wait to tell the FAO about it for the first time when you are appealing for an improved package (which we'll cover in Step 6), asking that the package not be reduced by the value of the outside scholarship. Be aware that this is not always possible; some schools have specific policies on this, while others are ready to be flexible. In some cases, we have seen FAOs let the parents use part of that money to reduce the family contribution, especially if the full financial need has not been met by the original aid package. In other cases, FAOs have agreed to use the scholarship to replace loan or work-study components of the package instead of grants from the school.

Onward! In the next chapter, we'll look at how to decode your financial aid award letter and how to determine which school is actually the better deal.

Decode Your Financial Aid Offer

First off, students, if you're reading this chapter: congratulations! You got in! That acceptance letter (or possibly letters!) is a sweet little summation of all of the work you've done, both before the admissions process began and throughout. You've earned it.

Now that your family is basking in the glow of a yes (or yeses), it's time to start thinking about the practicalities of the next four years, courtesy of the financial aid award letter that should arrive either alongside or soon after the acceptance; this is how the particular school's FAO suggests your need can be met. For the first time in awhile, you have all of the information at your fingertips—there's no mystery algorithms or institutional voodoo at play. The question is...how do you make sense of it?

Sifting the Offers

The week acceptance and award letters arrive can be very tough, as you are confronted with the economic realities of the different schools' offers. Your child's first choice school may have given you an aid package you cannot accept. The week will be immeasurably easier if you have taken the financial aid process into account when you were selecting schools to apply to in the first place so that backups (remember the financial safety school?) are in place, and expectations are established ahead of time.

In order to lock in your financial aid package and admission, most colleges will need a commitment before "Decision Day," traditionally May 1st. This gives you only a few weeks to contemplate and compare offers, and—if necessary—appeal for additional aid if the offered package puts the college beyond your financial reach.

What Makes up an Aid Package?

The details of an aid package will be spelled out in the award letter. This letter will tell you the total cost of one year's attendance at the college, what the college decided you could afford to pay toward that cost, and the package that the college has put together to meet your "need."

You'll remember from Step 1 that grants and scholarships are the all-stars of the aid package because they don't require repayment; we already drilled down into the more specific types of grants in Step 5. Let's rehash the package components one more time:

- **Grants:** Free money. A combination of government, state, and school-issued grants and scholarships, including Pell and SEOG.

- **Scholarships:** Also free money, although sometimes with caveats. The scholarships that appear in the award letter will usually be awarded by the school.

- **Federal Work-Study (FWS):** Government-subsidized part-time work for the student.

- **Student Loans:** Often government-subsidized loans, to be repaid after the student graduates.

Sample Award Letter

ANYTOWN UNIVERSITY
OFFICE OF FINANCIAL AID

Academic Year
2019-2020
Budget Assumptions
Resident Dependent Single
Identification Number
U123456709
Award Date
March 20, 2019

Joe Bloggs
123 Main Street
Sometown, ST 12345

NOTIFICATION OF FINANCIAL AID

After careful consideration, the Financial Aid Committee has authorized this offer of financial assistance for the award period indicated at left. The decision was made after careful consideration of your application.

To accept this award, you must complete, sign and return the white copy of this form within four weeks of receipt. This award is subject to cancellation if you do not respond by the specified date.

If you choose to decline any part of this offer, please place a check mark in the "DECLINED" box for the corresponding part of the package.

Be sure to review the terms and conditions of the award as described in the Financial Aid booklet enclosed.

DECLINED		FALL 2019	SPRING 2020
☐	Anytown University Scholarship	$11,975.00	$11,975.00
☐	Federal SEOG Grant	$500.00	$500.00
☐	Estimated Federal Pell Grant	$1,720.00	$1,720.00
☐	Recommended Federal Direct Loan	$1,750.00	$1,750.00
☐	Federal Work-Study	$665.00	$665.00
	TOTAL	$16,610.00	$16,610.00

FAMILY RESOURCES		SUMMARY	
Parent's Contribution	$980.00	Total Estimated Budget	$36,000.00
Student's Contribution	$1,800.00	Less: Family Contribution	$2,780.00
Other Resources	0.00	Financial Need	$33,220.00
TOTAL FAMILY CONTRIBUTION	$2,780.00	TOTAL FINANCIAL AID	$33,220.00

Jane Doe, Director

Source: Paying for College, 2019 edition, page 210

Note that in this case, the family contribution was set at $2,780. The total cost of attendance at Anytown for that year was $36,000. Thus, this family had a remaining "need" of roughly $33,220 which was—in this case—met in full with a mixture of grants, loans, and work-study.

The Bloggs were evidently a high-need family, and received an excellent package: $28,390 in grants (outright gift aid, which did not need to be repaid), $1,330 in work-study, and $3,500 in loans for the year.

Not all colleges will meet the entire remaining "need" of every student (see below), and there may have been a number of reasons why the package was so good in the case of the sample student in the report above. Perhaps Joe Bloggs was a violin prodigy, or the impoverished grandchild of a distinguished alumnus.

Unmet Need

If you'll recall, this is bad news—this is the school saying that they cannot meet your full financial need, and that there will be a "gap" between the cost of attendance and what you can pay plus the financial aid the school can offer.

Sometimes the colleges themselves will be willing to lend you the money to bridge that gap. Sometimes you will be able to take advantage of other loan programs such as the Federal Parent Loans for Undergraduate Students (PLUS), which is a partially-subsidized loan to parents of college students. The terms are less attractive than the subsidized student loans but still better than unsecured loans the banks would offer.

Federal Work-Study

Under this program, students are given part-time jobs (usually on campus) to help meet the family's remaining need. Many parents feel compelled to tell the student to reject the work-study portion of the aid package so as not to distract the student during the first year of classes. We suggest you wait to see what sort of work is being offered. Since students can almost always back out of work-study jobs at any time, why not see how taxing the job really is? Typically, students who work up to 10 hours a week actually show higher GPAs than those who work more or who don't work at all because they have to budget their time effectively.

While work-study wages are usually minimum wage or slightly higher, they carry the important added benefit of being exempt from the aid formulas; work-study wages do not count as part of the student's income in determining future aid eligibility. Other earnings, by contrast, may be assessed at a rate of up to 50 cents on the dollar. Not to mention, each dollar your child earns is a dollar you won't have to borrow. Work-study jobs are also great ways to earn hands-on skills that will prepare your child well for the job market—like managing social media for the university Admissions Office or conducting research in a lab for the university science department, for example. They also provide the student with an opportunity to develop a mentoring relationship with the department supervisor, which can be helpful for a future job reference.

Examples of Common Work Study Jobs vs. Quirky Work Study Jobs

They may all fall under the Federal Work-Study umbrella, but jobs can run the gamut.

Common work-study jobs found at all colleges can include:

Laboratory research assistant

Fitness/Student center receptionist

Library worker

Office administrative duties

Tutoring

Quirkier work-study jobs (definitely not found at all colleges) can include:

Welding shop assistant

Candy striper

Sexual Health educator

Sports announcer

Animal rescue shelter worker

Loans

There are plenty of kinds of college loans, but they mainly fall into two categories: need-based loans (designed to help meet part of a family's remaining need) and non-need-based loans (designed to help pay part of the family contribution when the family doesn't have the cash on hand). The loans you'll see in your aid package in the award letter are primarily need-based loans. We'll go into the different types of loans and their benefits in Step 7.

Financial Sleight of Hand

By their very nature, non-need-based loans should not appear as part of your need-based aid package. As far as the colleges are concerned, your family contribution is your business, and they don't have to help you to pay it. However, a number of schools do include several types of non-need-based loans in their aid package, (including PLUS and unsubsidized Direct loans).

As we said earlier, not all colleges can meet your full financial need. When a college tries to meet your need with a PLUS loan in the award letter, it is really covering the "gap" with a loan which you could have gotten anyway, as long as your credit held up. If you are offered a PLUS loan as part of your need-based aid, you should realize that the college has really not met your need in full. An aid package that includes a PLUS loan is not as valuable as a package that truly meets a family's remaining need.

> **TIP** **On Filing State Aid to the Correct College**
>
> If you have been awarded state aid at the school of your choice, but the award notice you received from the state agency lists the wrong college, you will have to file a form with the state agency to have the funds applied to the school you chose.

The Size of the Package Is Not As Important As the Potential Debt Load

Families often get swept up by the total value of the aid packages. We've heard parents say, "This school gave us $12,000 in aid, which is much better than the school that gave us only $7,000." The real measure of an aid package is how much YOU will have to end up paying, and how much debt the student will have to take on. Let's look at three examples:

*School A:
total cost—$30,000
family contribution—$11,000
grants and scholarships—$14,000
need-based loans—$3,000
work-study—$1,000
unmet need (what the parents will have to pay in addition to the family
    contribution)—$1,000
value of the aid package—$18,000
money the family will have to spend—$12,000
need-based debt—$3,000

School B:
total cost—$29,000
family contribution—$11,000
grants and scholarships—$17,000
need-based loans—$500
work-study—$500
unmet need—$0
value of the aid package—$18,000
money the family will have to spend—$11,000
need-based debt—$500

School C:
total cost—$25,000
family contribution—$10,500
grants and scholarships—$10,750
need-based loans—$3,250
work-study—$500
unmet need—$0
value of the aid package—$14,500
money the family will have to spend—$10,500
need-based debt—$3,250

*Source: Paying for College, 2019 edition, pages 223-24

School A and school B gave identical total dollar amounts in aid, but the two packages were very different. School B gave $17,000 in grants (which do not have to be repaid), while A gave only $14,000. School B would actually cost this family $11,000 with only $500 in student loans. School A would cost the family $12,000 with $3,000 in student loans. Leaving aside for the moment subjective matters such as the academic caliber of the two schools, school B was a better buy.

School C would cost this family $10,500 in cash. On the other hand, this school also asked the student to take on the largest amount of debt: $3,250.

You've probably noticed that the sticker prices of the three colleges were almost totally irrelevant to the breakdown. After you've looked at the bottom line for each of the colleges in contention, you should also factor in the academic quality of the schools; perhaps it is worth a slightly higher price to send your child to a school that has higher graduation and career placement rates or to one that has a better "reputation." You should also look at factors like location and reputation of the department your child is interested in, not to mention the student's preference. In the end, you'll have to choose what price you're willing to pay for what level of quality.

CHART: Average financial aid awards (private, state) (2014-15)

Private university (4-year):

89.5% awarded financial aid

32.6% received federal grants (average award: $4,826)

25.9% received state/local grants (average award: $3,842)

82.4% received institutional grants (average award: $17,845)

60.9% took out student loans (average award: $8,003)

Public university (4-year):

83.5% awarded financial aid

37.5% received federal grants (average award: $4,669)

37.6% received state/local grants (average award: $3,842)

47.2% received institutional grants (average award: $5,648)

49.5% took out student loans (average award: $6,698)

Appealing for a Better Aid Package

Even if a school's award letter has left you with a package you cannot accept—maybe the amount of student loan money is too high, or maybe your need simply just wasn't met—you may still be able to appeal for additional assistance. Over the past few years we've noticed the initial aid offer, especially at some of the more selective schools, has become a lot more subjective to adjustment.

Many parents feel understandably battle-scarred by the aid process and don't want to go back to the table. However, if the aid package won't allow you to send your child to that school, what is there to lose? Most FAOs will appreciate learning that they are about to risk losing a qualified applicant solely because of money.

The key to a successful appeal is to be friendly, firm, and in control. Have a number in your head and be able to back it up with documentation as to why the aid package the school has provided just won't work (maybe even use other school's more preferable packages for illustration), and the FAO just might make it so that it does.

TIP **The Worst They Can Say Is No**

You risk nothing by appealing for a better package. No matter how objectionable you as a parent are, the school cannot take back their offer of admission, and the FAOs cannot take back their aid package unless you have lied about your financial details.

Not Everyone Should Hustle for More Money

We are most definitely not advising every family to try to get more money. If you can comfortably afford the amount the college says you must pay, there is little chance the school is going to throw more cash your way—the aid package must be pretty good already. College FAOs know just how fair the package they have put together for you is. If you are being greedy, you will not get much sympathy. It's also fair to remember that the average FAO isn't making a great deal of money, so whining about having to eke out an existence on $200,000 a year won't elicit much sympathy.

However, if you are facing the real prospect of not being able to send your child to the school she really wants to attend because of money, or if two similarly ranked colleges have offered radically different packages and your son really wants to go to the school with the lower package, then you should sit down and map out your strategy.

Appeal While You Still Have Leverage

After you've accepted the college's offer of admission, the college won't have much incentive to grant your appeal, so you should plan to speak to the FAO while it's still apparent you might go elsewhere. Similarly, you will not have much leverage if you show the FAO a rival offer from a college that is ranked considerably lower than the college of choice.

Try to make an objective assessment of how badly the college wants you. FAOs are well aware where each student fits into their scheme of things. A student that just barely squeaked in is going to have a lot less bargaining power than a shining star.

The Call

Unless you live within driving distance of the school, you're going to want to pick up the phone. The FAOs will find it hard to believe that you need more money if you can afford to fly to their college just to complain.

If possible, try to speak with the head FAO or one of the head FAO's assistants. Make sure you write down the name of the person with whom you spoke. It is unlikely that he will make a concession on the telephone, so don't be disappointed if he says he will have to get back to you or asks you to send him something in writing.

Some Tips to Keep in Mind:

- Have a number in your head. What would you like to get out of this conversation? If the FAO asks you, "All right, how much can you afford?" you do not want to hesitate.

- Be reasonable. If the family contribution you propose has no relation to your EFC, you will lose most of your credibility with the FAO.

- Avoid confrontational language. Rather than start off with, "Match my other offer or else," ask if there is anything they can do to improve the package. Also avoid using words such as "negotiate" or "bargain" and instead say you wish to "appeal" the package.

- If you are near a deadline, ask for an extension and be doubly sure you know the name of the person with whom you are speaking. Follow up with a letter (certified mail, return receipt requested) reminding the FAO of what was discussed in the conversation.

- Parents, not students, should speak with the FAOs because it is the parent who will, for the most part, be paying the bill.

Key questions and phrases to use in your FAO appeal call

"We received your award letter and though we appreciate the aid, we'd like to appeal the package."

"In looking at our finances, we need (specific, reasonable number of dollars) in order for (student) to be able to attend"

"(School) is my son's first choice, and the whole family really wants him to be able to attend."

When asking for more money, be sure to mention:

-That the family has planned and budgeted for college all along

-Any specific reason why more money is needed (either a change since filing the FAFSA, or any circumstances that might not have been apparent on paper)

-You are prepared to borrow to pay for college

-Any academic improvements or notable achievements that have taken place during the student's senior year

As a last resort:

You can mention that another college (or college) has offered a more generous package, but don't lie - you may be required to submit a copy of the award letter.

Prepare Your Ammunition

Before you call, you gather all of the documents and reasons supporting your request for more money. These could include:

✔ Better offers from a comparable school (be prepared to send a copy of the rival award letter)

✔ Evidence of special circumstances not taken into account by the aid formula (such as high margin debts, support of an elderly relative, or unusually high unreimbursed business expenses)

✔ Any change in your circumstances since you filled out the need analysis forms (for example, you have recently separated, divorced, been widowed, or lost your job)

Choosing a School and Accepting an Award

The time has come to pick a horse in the race! After the student and parent(s) have received all acceptance letters, compared aid packages, and have discussed the pros, cons, and economic feasibility of attending each school, it's time to make the choice.

It's important to note that you should not accept a school's offer of admission by posting an enrollment deposit UNLESS you are prepared also to accept the financial aid award. This must be completed by May 1, which means if you are appealing an aid offer, do so early so that you have time to receive a response and then to pay the deposit by May 1. You should accept the aid award at the same time. Do not accept and an award prior to accepting the offer of admission. Do not reject any aid offer until you have made your final choice of a college.

> **TIP** **Send It Certified**
>
> If you send in your financial aid acceptance letter by mail, always send via certified mail with return receipt requested. Many colleges today have online acceptance forms. Be sure to print yours out as proof of submission.

Should You Turn Down Any Parts of an Aid Package?

Some parents worry that by turning down part of the financial aid package they are endangering future aid, as if by refusing a work-study job or a need-based loan, you're signaling to the FAOs that you can find the money elsewhere. This is actually a valid worry. There really aren't many times when it would be a good idea for a family to turn down grants, scholarships, need-based loans, or work-study. Even if you do find reason to turn down part of an aid package, you certainly shouldn't do so before you've compared all of the packages you've received as a group to determine your options.

We can't think of many times it'd be a good idea for a family to turn down grants, scholarships, need-based loans, or work-study, but the exceptions might include:

- If a student needs to focus entirely on their studies and feels work-study would distract from that (although we have found that working a reasonable number of hours—usually no more than 10 a week – forces students to budget their time better)

- If the amount of loans are in surplus of what is needed (to avoid paying interest on extraneous funds), although there is no interest on subsidized loans while the student is in college

- If the contingencies of a specific scholarship are too daunting or complicated to be worth the amount of the award

Is the Package Renewable?

Most colleges will say that need-based aid packages will stay roughly the same for all four years assuming that your financial situation remains relatively the same. Students also must maintain what is known as Satisfactory Academic Progress toward a degree, based both on a minimum GPA and the accumulation of credits. These are very minimum standards that most students will meet, but you should ask the FAO about them as they can differ among schools. No matter what, you'll be reapplying for aid every year until graduation. With respect to merit aid, every college will set its own policies, so be sure to ask if there is a minimum GPA required for scholarship renewal and what, if any, grace periods are allowed.

Bait and Switch

Most reputable colleges don't indulge in bait-and-switch tactics, whereby students are lured to the school with a sensational financial aid package that promptly disappears the next year.

When parents feel they have been victims of bait and switch, there has often been some kind of misunderstanding. This might occur when parents have two children in school at the same time. If one of the children graduates, the parents are often surprised when the EFC for the child who remains in college goes up dramatically. This is not bait and switch. The family now has more available income and assets to pay for the child who is now in college alone.

Additionally, schools sometimes minimize work-study hours during the first year so that students have a chance to get accustomed to college life. Parents are often surprised when the number of work-study hours is increased the second year, but it is reasonable to expect students to work more hours in their junior and senior years.

Now That You Have Chosen a School

By the time you've said yes to a college, it'll already be halfway through your second base income year. Now that you understand the ins and outs of financial aid, you can plan ahead to minimize the apparent size of your income and assets, and be in an even better position to fill out next year's need analysis forms to maximize aid. The first application for financial aid is the hardest, in part because you're dealing with a number of different schools and an unknown formula. From now on, that first application will serve as a kind of template.

STEP SEVEN

Be Realistic About Debt

Ideally, the student got into her first choice college, which promptly provided an acceptable financial aid package that met all of the family's need through grants, scholarships, and work study. Or perhaps, a rich great uncle who values the pursuit of higher education stepped in to cover any difference between grants and scholarships and the cost of tuition. But....we know that might not be the case.

The truth is, a significant proportion of financial aid packages comes in the form of loans. They are a well-trod reality of obtaining a degree, and can be a bane to students and parents for years to come, but they are a necessary burden. However, you're a smart family who have clearly thought in the financial long term (and bought this book!), and should be able to minimize the hardship of having to take out loans.

If you'll remember from Step 6, the loans you receive will fall into two categories: need-based, and non-need-based loans. Much like the schools to which the student has applied to, these loans will appeal to the family in a distinct order of attractiveness.

 Never put tuition on a credit card.

The debt is more expensive than ever given recent changes to interest rates and other fees some card issuers are now charging.

Need-Based Loans

The best need-based loan (the federally subsidized Direct Loan, which we'll go into more in a bit) is such a good deal in terms of interest rates that families should almost always accept them if offered. In most cases, no interest is charged while the student is in school, and repayment does not begin on Direct Loans until the student graduates, leaves college, or dips below half-time status.

Even if you have the money in the bank, we'd suggest taking the loans, so your money can earn interest while your student is in college. When the loans come due, you can pay them off in full, without penalty. Most college loans have an origination fee. The current (2018-19) Direct Loan origination fee is 1.062%. For Direct PLUS Loans, the fee is 4.248%. These fees are deducted from the value of the loan itself; and you will never have to pay them out of your pocket but you will be responsible for repaying the full loan amount including the fee.

> **TIP** **How Much Can You Borrow?**
>
> Undergraduates can borrow up to $5,500 for the first year $6500 for the second year, and $7500 for each of the third and fourth years of college, with a cap of $31,000, with no more than $23,000 in subsidized loans.

Federal Direct Loans

Sometimes known as the William D. Ford Federal Direct Loans, there are two kinds of Direct loans. The better kind is the subsidized Direct loan. To get this, a student must be judged to have need by the college. The federal government then subsidizes the loan by not charging any interest until after the student graduates, leaves college, or goes below half-time attendance status. The current (2018-19) interest rate on subsidized (and unsubsidized) Direct Loans is 5.05%.

The second kind of Direct loan is known as unsubsidized and is not based on need, so the student will be charged interest from the start. Students are given the option of paying the interest while in school, or deferring the interest payments (which will continue to accrue) until repayment of principle begins. Virtually all students who fill out a FAFSA are eligible for these unsubsidized Direct loans.

The federal government guarantees the loan, and if applicable, makes up any difference between the student's low interest rate and the prevailing market rate once repayment has begun. A dependent student may be eligible to borrow up to $5,500 for the freshman year, up to $6,500 for the sophomore year, and up to $7,500 per year for the remaining undergraduate years. However for all of these annual limits, at least $2,000 must be unsubsidized in any year.

 Borrowing Beyond Need

If a student is awarded a subsidized Direct loan but the amount is less than the maximum subsidized amount, the student can accept the subsidized loan to meet her need, and then also take out an unsubsidized Direct loan for the remainder of the total annual borrowing limit.

The College's Own Loans

These loans can be all over the board in terms of appeal and sensibility. Some are incredibly generous: Princeton University offers special loans for parents at very low rates. Some are not so good: a few colleges have loan programs that require almost immediate repayment with interest rates that rival VISA and MasterCard. While these types of loans do not normally appear as part of an aid package, a few colleges may include them as part of an aid package. Remember that you are allowed to reject any portion of the aid package, and you should always carefully look at the terms of college-supplied loans before accepting them.

> **TIP** **Thinking Ahead to Grad School**
>
> Those considering going on to graduate or professional school should borrow the maximum amount of subsidized Direct Loans for which they are eligible. Even if you'd rather not borrow, because interest is not charged on subsidized direct loans while you are in college, you're better off using these loans and preserving funds in your bank account while an undergraduate, so that you can use them in graduate school, when the cost of borrowing is higher.

Non-Need-Based Loans

While the other types of college loans won't be part of your aid package, they are certainly relevant, because you might be wondering how you're going to pay your EFC for the next four years as you peruse the various college aid packages. So here's the truth: most families end up borrowing.

There are so many different loans offered by banks and organizations that you wouldn't be able to lift this book if we were to list them. College bulletins usually include information about the types of loans available at the school, but what follows are some of the more mainstream alternatives (we'll talk about a few of the more offbeat ways of paying for college in Step 8).

Keep in mind, the PLUS loan (Parent Loan for Undergraduate Students) is probably the best of all these options. Unless you are able to secure more favorable terms from a state financing authority's alternative education loan program, then the only reasons to consider other types of non-need-based loans besides the PLUS loan are if you prefer having the loans in the student's name.

> **TIP** **Try not to take money from a retirement account or 401(k) to pay for college.**
>
> In addition to likely early distribution penalties and additional income taxes, the higher income will reduce your aid eligibility.

PLUS Loans

As far as credit-based loans go, the PLUS is probably the best. Parents can borrow up to the annual total cost of attendance at the college minus any financial aid received. With all PLUS loans now disbursed via the Direct Loan Program, you will apply for the PLUS loan through the financial aid office. The current (2018-19) fixed interest rate on the PLUS loan is 7.6% with an origination fee of 4.248%.

Many parents worry their credit rating is not good enough to get a PLUS loan; before you automatically assume you won't qualify, you should realize that the credit test for the PLUS is not as stringent as it is for most other loans, and you don't need to have excellent credit to qualify. You basically just can't have an "adverse credit history" (i.e. outstanding judgments, liens, extremely slow payments). Even if you fail the credit check, there are still exceptions made for extenuating circumstances, or borrowers who can find acceptable co-signers. If a parent is denied a PLUS loan, the undergraduate dependent student may be eligible for additional an unsubsidized loan of up to $4,000. The FAO will have more information about how to obtain these "PLUS-Deny" funds through a program dubbed Supplemental Loan for Students (SLS).

> **TIP** **PLUS Loans are for Parents**
>
> Administered by the government, the PLUS loan is made to parents of undergraduate college children. Virtually any parent can get a PLUS loan of up to the total cost of attendance minus any financial aid received—provided the federal government thinks the parent is a good credit risk.

Alternative State Loans

Some states make guaranteed student loans available. These are sometimes called "special loans." If your state offers these loans and if you qualify, they will appear as part of your aid package. The terms vary from state-to-state; some are available only to students, others only to parents; many are below market rate. Unlike state grants, state loans are often available to non-residents attending approved colleges in that state.

Lines of Credit

Some banks offer revolving credit loans that do not start accruing interest until you write a check on the line of credit.

CitiAssist Loans

Sponsored by Citibank, these loans (to students) do not have any origination fees. To make up for this, the interest rate is usually prime plus 0.50 percent (however this may be lower or higher at some schools). This is one of the few loan programs available to foreign students who can borrow funds by having a credit-worthy co-signer (who must be a U.S. citizen or permanent resident). Co-signers will also be required for almost all undergraduates as well as those students who do not have a positive credit history. Under certain circumstances, the co-signer can be released from the loan after forty-eight on-time payments are made.

Sallie Mae Smart Option Student Loans

These co-signed private student loans require payment of interest while the student is in school and during the six-month separation period before repayment. Co-signers may not be required after the first year. The interest rate is pegged to the prime rate and will vary depending on the credit rating of the student/co-signer, as well as the school itself. This program offers a 0.25 percent interest rate reduction for students who elect to have their payments made automatically through their bank and a 0.25 percent interest rate reduction for students who receive all servicing communications via a valid e-mail address.

Collegiate Loans

Wells Fargo Bank operates this non-need-based program for college which offers variable interest loans currently based on the prime rate and your credit history. The student is the borrower, but a parent and/or another individual usually must co-sign. One can normally borrow up to the cost of education minus any financial aid.

Before You Borrow

How do you decide which type of loan to take out? Consider all of the following questions:

- What is the interest rate and how is it determined?

- Is the interest rate fixed or variable, and if variable, is there a cap?

- What are the repayment options? How many years will it take to pay off the loan? Can you make interest-only payments while the child is in school? Can you repay the loan early?

- Who is the borrower—the parent or the student?

- Are there origination fees?

- Is a co-signer permitted or required?

- Will having a co-signer affect the interest rate and/or origination fees?

- Is the loan secured or unsecured? The rates on a loan secured by the home or by securities are generally lower, but you are putting your assets on the line.

- Is the interest on the loan tax-deductible?

Before You Borrow, Look at Rates

For many people, there is no other option; if your child wants a college education, you have to go into debt. But it turns out that there are a number of choices to make about how you go into debt, and how you eventually pay it off. If you do need to borrow in order to finance college, there is no way to avoid the piper eventually knocking at your door, but what you can do is select the best loans in terms or repayment.

If you have to borrow, first pursue federal education loans, and avoid private loans if you can. Let's look at the repayment math behind some of the types of federal loans we just covered.

Subsidized Direct Loans

It's safe to assume that you should always borrow at the lowest possible cost, so the first type of loan to consider is usually the subsidized Direct Loan to the student that we covered earlier in the chapter— Dependent on the 10-year Treasury Note rate, the Direct Loan currently carries a 5.05% fixed-interest; interest is subsidized while the student is in school, and during a six-month grace period after the student leaves school, graduates, or drops below half-time status.

If you wish to pay off a subsidized Direct Loan before the student leaves school, graduates, or drops below half-time enrollment, no interest will be charged at all. Remember, Direct Loans carry an origination fee of 1.062%.

Unsubsidized Direct Loans

Next in desirability is the unsubsidized Direct Loan. Unlike the subsidized Direct Loan, the unsubsidized Direct Loan charges the student interest (the same 5.05% as for the subsidized loan) from day one, so the decision to take out this type of loan depends on other factors. For example, let's say you have funds for school in a bank account that's earning 1 percent in a bank; in that case, it makes no sense to take out a loan in which you're paying more interest than you're earning by keeping those funds in a bank. On the flip side, if you don't have the funds to pay for school, and other loans would carry a higher interest rate, then the unsubsidized Direct Loan makes sense.

Private Alternative Loans

There are two other types of loans available which can be broken down into two categories: alternative state loans mentioned earlier, and private alternative loans, generally offered by banks or other private lenders—of which you should be wary.

While these mostly variable rate loans can start out lower than the Federal options, if interest rates rise appreciably they can become very costly. And unlike housing debt, in which you can convert a variable rate home equity line of credit into a fixed-rate loan before interest rates start to rise, these education loans normally cannot be refinanced with another fixed-rate education loan.

How to Pay Off Your Loans

The repayment clock starts pretty much as soon as you flip that graduation cap tassel. The government gives you a six-month grace period to find a job and catch your breath—and then the bills start arriving. It might seem like this part is painful but simple, but there are actually a bewildering number of repayment options, not to mention chances to postpone and defer payment.

There is one simple thing to remember: The longer you take to pay, the more it costs you. Choosing to lower your monthly payments will stretch out the amount of time you'll be making these payments, and ultimately adds a ton of interest to your bill.

The only way to defer these student loan payments long-term is to stay in school. As long as you are at least a half-time student at an approved post-secondary school, you can keep those bills at bay forever. If you get a job and then later decide to go on to graduate school, your loan payments may be deferred while you are in graduate school, and resume as soon as you get out.

The National Student Loan Data System

It can be hard to keep track of exactly how much debt a student has accrued, and what needs to be paid back and when. Fortunately, there is a database of information about federally funded loans and grants awarded to students—the National Student Loan Data System (NSLDS). Schools send your loan information into the NSLDS, so it's straight from the horse's mouth.

If a student has registered for an FSA ID (and they should! See Step 4), then they can access their entire federal education loan history via the NSLDS, which also breaks down the type of loan between subsidized and unsubsidized loans. Through the NSLDS, students can view all of their loans and grants during their complete life cycle, from aid approval through disbursement, repayment, deferment, delinquency, and closure. As the student starts to consolidate or pay off their loans, he can check in and see the figure beside each loans dwindle.

The Different Payment Plans

If you are repaying Direct Loans, Supplemental Loans for Students (SLS), PLUS, or Grad PLUS loans, there are up to seven repayment options at present. When you pick an option, it is not for life—you can switch at any time. Here is a brief summary of the options, but be sure to contact your FAO and visit https://studentaid.ed.gov/sa/node/78 for full details before choosing.

- **Standard repayment:** The loans must be repaid in equal installments spread out over up to ten years. This is a good plan for people who have relatively little debt, or have enough income to afford the relatively high payments.

- **Extended repayment:** Loan payments may be fixed or graduated over a period that can extend up to twenty-five years. The increased time period reduces monthly payments, but long-term interest expenses go up dramatically. Students must have more than $30,000 in Direct Loans to be eligible for this plan.

- **Graduated repayment:** Loan payments start out low and increase over time to ensure that your loan will be repaid within 10 years. The payments must always at least equal the monthly interest that's accruing. This is a good plan for young people whose earnings are low, but are expected to increase over time. Over the lifetime of the loan, interest expenses are much higher.

- **Income contingent repayment:** This option is available only to borrowers with federal Direct Loans, but does not cover parent PLUS loans. In this plan, the payments are based on a combination of the borrower's level of debt and current income. With this (and the following two options), payments can be lower than the monthly interest accruing (which is called negative amortization). Of course, this can add substantially to the final cost of long-term interest expenses. To counter this, at the end of twenty-five years, the government will forgive any unpaid balance; however, the IRS may tax you on this unpaid balance).

- **Income-based repayment and Pay As You Earn:** Under these options, the required monthly payment will be based on your income during any period when you have a partial financial hardship. The monthly payment may be adjusted annually. The maximum repayment period under these plans may exceed ten years. If you meet certain requirements over a specified period of time, you may qualify for cancellation of any outstanding balance after twenty years. The amount of any loan canceled may be subject to income taxes. Parent PLUS Loans are not eligible. Only Direct Loans qualify for Pay As You Earn.

**Typical 10-year standard loan repayment schedule
for average debt (federal student loans)**

After graduation:

One day: Grace period begins

6 months: 120 payments commence

Private (average loan: $8,003):

Monthly Loan Payment: $92.10

Cumulative Payments: $11,051.79

Total Interest Paid: $3,048.79

Public (average loan: $6,698):

Monthly Loan Payment: $77.08

Cumulative Payments: $9,249.74

Total Interest Paid: $2,551.74

Loan Consolidation

Government regulations allow you to consolidate all your education loans from different sources into one big loan—often with lower monthly payments than you were making before. As usual, the catch is that the repayment period is extended, meaning that you end up paying a lot more in interest over the increased life of the loan. However, you can always prepay your loans without penalty.

The loans that can be consolidated are: the Stafford and Perkins Loans (these have been discontinued), Direct Loans, SLS (when parents do not qualify for PLUS), PLUS loans, GradPLUS loans, and loans issued by the government's programs for health care professionals. You cannot consolidate private loans from colleges or other sources in the federal consolidation program.

How It Works

A consolidation loan can be paid back using one of the plans outlined above. Loan consolidation isn't always the smartest route—for example, if you are almost done paying off your loans. For the most part, student loans can be consolidated only once, and it's almost always best to wait until the student is completely finished with school.

Also: you don't have to consolidate all your loans. The rules on how your new interest rate will be calculated change constantly, so you'll need to get up-to-date information from your lender.

Before you consolidate any loans, you should also consider these factors:

- How will the interest rate be calculated?

- Are you better off excluding some loans from consolidation to get a better rate and/or to prevent the loss of some benefits with some of your loans?

- Will consolidating your loans later give you a better or a worse interest rate?

- Can you consolidate your loans(s) more than once?

- Do you have to consolidate your loans with a private lender? Do you have to consolidate your loans directly with the government? If you have a choice between the two, which consolidation plan is the best deal for you?

- If you are consolidating unsubsidized and subsidized loans together, will this affect your ability to have the government pay the interest on your subsidized loans should you go back to school?

Loan Discharge and Cancellation

Direct Loans have various provisions in which the loan can be discharged or canceled. While some provisions hopefully do not happen to you in the near future (e.g. you become permanently disabled or die), loans may also be forgiven for performing certain types of service (teaching in low-income areas, working in public sector jobs in the government, the military, certain non-profit tax-exempt organizations, law enforcement, public health, or education, may be eligible—after making 120 on-time payments—to have the remaining balance of their Direct Loans forgiven.

> **TIP** **The Smartest Loan Strategy? Prepayment.**
>
> All federal education loans can be prepaid without any penalty. This means that by paying even a little more than your monthly payment, you can pay off the loan much faster than you might have thought possible, and save yourself a bundle in interest. If you're going to do this, try to prepay the loans with the highest interest rates first.

Above All, Avoid Default

It can take years to build up a good credit rating again once you've screwed it up, and you may not be able to get credit cards, a mortgage, or even cable in the meantime. There are so many different payment options, that there's no need for anyone ever to default on their loans.

If you lose a job, or "encounter economic hardship," you should apply for a temporary deferment (suspension of principal and interest payments for a specified time) or something called forbearance, which can include temporary suspension of payments, a time extension, or even a temporary reduction in the amount of monthly installments. Many lenders will draw up new repayment plans, or accept a missed payment as long as you inform them ahead of time.

Funding Your Future: Get Creative

All right: you've saved and shuffled your money, filed all the financial aid and scholarship applications, compared aid packages and called the FAOs, and selected the most sensible federal loans, all to make sure you're getting every last cent that's coming to you. Surely there's nothing more that can be done beyond packing up the car, right?

Whether you see this as a positive or not...there is! You may have locked down tuitions and interest rates and scholarships, but one thing still within parents' and student's control is how the student's time at the college is spent. Obviously less time in school is going to save on tuition and living costs, but there are other ways to cut corners or get the most bang for your buck while in school so as to reduce debts post-graduation. Not every school is going to have all—or even any—of these options, but there might still be a few tricks left in the bag to save money.

Get Good Grades and High SAT/ACT Scores

Working toward great grades and test scores is a very tangible way a student can help pay for college.

Study Like Crazy

Good grades can make a student desirable to colleges. Yes, a great GPA can help you get in, but in these budget-tight times, good grades also translate directly into dollars and cents. A high GPA in a very demanding curriculum can qualify a student for a higher merit-based award.

Even at the most slective schools, where students are awarded aid based only on their "need," applicants with high academic achievement do get preferential packages—awards with a higher percentage of grants (which don't have to be paid back) and a lower percentage of loans (which definitely do).

There are some colleges out there who state up front, "If you have a GPA of more than 3.5 and SATs of 1300 or above, we will offer you a full tuition scholarship." There are other schools (more and more in recent years) that give out large merit-based scholarships, irrespective of need. These grants are not necessarily just for geniuses. There are more than a few colleges that award merit-based grants to students with B averages.

Take an SAT/ACT Review Course

Nothing can change a student's fortune faster than a big increase or SAT or ACT. Look at this way: it takes four years to accumulate your grades from high school. It takes six weeks to take a prep course. A study by FAIRTEST, published in *The New York Times*, showed that students who took these prep courses had an average improvement of over 100 points.

Every 10 points a student can raise his score on the SAT can save his family money by increasing his desirability in the eyes of the financial aid officers and increasing the size of the scholarships or grants offered to him. This is too important to leave to chance.

There are many companies that offer test preparation, some affordable and some quite expensive. We, of course, are partial to The Princeton Review in person and online courses and tutors. If there are no preparation courses offered in your area, we suggest you at least buy a book such as The Princeton Review's *Cracking the ACT* or *Cracking the SAT*. Books such as these will provide the student with actual SAT practice tests and drills in addition to strategies. If money is a consideration, don't lose heart. The books are available at libraries, and test prep companies often offer financial aid. The Princeton Review offers online Self-Paced for the SAT, ACT, and PSAT (all three included!) starting at $99. Learn more at PrincetonReview.com/SAT

Condensing Your College Education

There are extremes to the "time equals money" approach to tuition. On one hand, if the student is motivated (and a little nuts), it is sometimes possible to complete a four-year education in three years. Since some schools charge by the credit, the family may not see big savings on the tuition itself (unless the student brings in AP credits from high school or from classes taken at a community college), but there will be savings on room and board, and the student will be able to get out in the workforce that much sooner.

However, there are some more reasonable goals that can help students reduce time in college; for instance, by attending summer school (which is often less expensive than the regular terms) a student can reduce her time on campus by a full semester.

 Don't rush

Even smaller reductions in time can take their toll on the student. Academics are only one part of the college experience, and by accelerating the process, a student may lose out on some of the opportunities and friendships that make the college years meaningful.

Take AP Courses

Many high schools offer advanced placement (AP) courses—which, purely from an admissions standpoint, are a good idea anyway. By passing an AP test at the end of the year, a student can earn college credits without paying college tuition, or at least place into higher level classes. Not all schools accept AP credits, but many do, again enabling a student to save his family literally thousands of dollars. Some students are able to skip their entire first year in this way—that's 25 percent less college costs to pay. Consult with the colleges you are interested in to see if they accept AP credits.

Earning Credits on the CLEP Exams

The College Board has developed exams that—like AP tests—allow students who score high enough to earn college credits, which could potentially save thousands in tuition. These are offered under the College-Level Examination Program, more commonly known as CLEP. There are currently thirty-three different CLEP exams, with at least one of them currently accepted by 2,900 colleges and universities. You earn the same number of credits you would earn by taking a course—simply by taking a test.

Obviously, you need to do your homework first. Some colleges don't award credits for CLEP exams at all, while others have fine print. It is up to the individual college to determine which exams can be taken, the minimum score you need in order to get credit, and the total number of credits the school is willing to give students for CLEP exams. Bear in mind that the minimum score needed on one test might be different than the minimum score on another test (each of which costs $80 to take). And some colleges might not give you credit, but will use the test results to allow you to place out of entry-level courses or to fulfill core distribution requirements.

> **TIP** **Does your school offer a dual enrollment program?**
>
> It is also possible to earn college credit via "dual enrollment" programs available at some high schools. These allow students to take college level courses during their senior year.

Adjusting the Four-Year Timeline

While four years used to be a given calendar for a degree, times have a-changed, and now plenty of schools offer alternate timeline structures—both abbreviated and extended—to accommodate the realities of getting a degree (for both traditional and non-traditional students).

Go to School Part-Time

Some schools allow students to attend college part-time so they can earn money while they are studying. It might seem odd to immediately suggest the opposite of condensing a college education, but this can be a great option for the right situation (particularly for students living at home). There are a few key things to be aware of before deciding this route:

- Student loans become due as early as six months after the student stops taking classes or goes below half-time status. If the student takes too much time off between classes, she may have to start paying off the loans, even though she's still in school.

- The financial aid available for part-time students is greatly reduced. If the student is attending less than half-time, there will be especially little chance of substantial aid.

- Any money the student earns is going to be assessed by the colleges at a very high rate, thus reducing aid eligibility. You should carefully consider whether a job will actually help pay for college. It will depend on whether your family was judged eligible for aid, and what kind of package you have been offered. If you were not eligible, or if the aid package left you with a substantial piece of "unmet need," then part-time study may make sense.

A good safeguard is to ask the FAO what would happen if the student earned, say, $15,000 after taxes this year. Would the student's aid package remain the same, or would the extra income simply reduce the aid package by $4,000 or more?

Transfer in Later

If a family is on a very tight budget, a good way to finance a four-year college education is to do part of it elsewhere, where the costs are much more manageable and the end result—a degree from a reputable institution—is still the same. This is not to say that the name on the diploma is all that matters, but the higher level classes at an institution (i.e. those usually taken in the third and fourth years) are usually where a school's academic mettle really comes through.

Note that this scenario won't work without an outstanding academic record. Prestigious private colleges will almost certainly not be interested in a transfer student with a B average or less. The other thing to bear in mind is that aid packages to transfer students are generally not as generous as those given to incoming first years.

Transferring from a Community College to a State College

Two-year public community colleges or junior colleges, where the average in-state tuition for 2017–2018 according to the College Board was just $3,570, represent an outstanding way to save money. A student with a good academic record at a community college (perhaps earned while still living at home and working) can then transfer to a more expensive state college for two more years to earn a BA. The total cost would be only a fraction of the cost of a private college, and still thousands of dollars less than that of a four-year program at the state college.

> **TIP** **Plan ahead.**
>
> Be sure the college you plan to transfer to will accept your community college credits.

Transferring from a Public College to a Private College

If a student really has their heart set on a particular private college but the family can't afford the cost of four years' tuition, the student could also go to a public college for the first two years and then transfer into the private school; the student will get the private college degree at a much more affordable price.

Obviously, the student would have to get accepted by the private school as a transfer student, and this can be quite difficult. Top grades are a must. It should be noted that while transfers into private colleges range from "not possible" to "routine", there is a whole set of likelihoods along the way. A student will usually have much better odds transferring from a state school instead of a community college.

Defer Admission

Many schools allow students to defer admission for a year, during which the student can earn money. We keep hammering this home, but always remember that at the moment, student earnings above a certain dollar amount will reduce aid eligibility—thus for many students, this strategy could backfire. However, if the college the student really wishes to attend decides the family is not eligible for aid and the family cannot shoulder the entire cost of college, this might be the only way the student could make up the difference.

Be extremely careful in making a decision like this. If there is no sensible plan for paying four years' worth of college bills, it may not make sense to begin the first year. As with going to school part-time while working, it is heavily advised to check with the school's FAO as to what would happen to the student's aid package in regards to any income earned in the gap year.

> **TIP** **Stick to your college and your major.**
>
> Changing colleges can result in lost credits. Aid may be limited/not available for transfer students at some schools. Changing majors can mean paying for extra courses to meet requirements.

Innovative Options

We've covered the mainstream borrowing options and methods for paying for college, but there's still further to go off the beaten path. Throughout the decades, colleges, private companies, public organizations, and smart individuals have come up with even more alternative ways to pay for college. These ideas range from the commonsense to the high-tech, from straightforward to labyrinthine. Here are just a few.

Cooperative Education

Over 900 colleges let students combine a college education with a job in their field. Generally, the students spend alternate terms attending classes full-time and then working full-time at off-campus jobs with private companies or the federal government, although some students work and study at the same time. The students earn money for tuition while getting practical hands-on experience in their areas of interest. This program differs from the Federal Work-Study Program in which the subsidized campus-based jobs are probably not related to the student's course of study, and take up far fewer hours. After graduating, a high percentage of cooperative education students get hired permanently by the employers they worked for during school. Companies from every conceivable field participate in this program. The federal government is the largest employer of cooperative education students.

Getting a degree through the cooperative education program generally takes about five years, but students have a big head start over similar-aged students; they already have valuable experience and a prospective employer in their field. They owe less money in student loans, and they are often paid more than a new hire.

If you are eligible for financial aid, you should contact the financial aid office at any college you are considering to determine the effect of cooperative earnings on your financial aid package.

Schools known for/requiring cooperative education assignments

- Boston University

- Carnegie Mellon University

- Drexel University

- Emory University

- Florida State University

- George Washington University

- Marquette University

- Northeastern University

- Pace University

- Pennsylvania State University—University Park

- University of Colorado Boulder

- University of Connecticut

- University of Missouri

- University of Southern California

- Vassar College

- Virginia Tech

- Wellesley College

4+1 Programs

An increasing number of colleges are now offering an accelerated five-year two-degree program known as 4+1—simplified, that's four years for a bachelor's degree and one year for a master's (there is overlap within, though). While the earning potential of a student with a higher degree is greater, and savings can be found in shaving a year or two off of the time it traditionally takes to get a master's degree following college, research still needs to be done. Not all colleges have 4+1 programs, and it's not always the case that the financial aid package awarded to the undergraduate years will carry over into the +1.

Students typically apply to these programs in their junior year, and they are not available in all areas of study. If a student thinks that they might want to pursue this track, they might need to already be thinking about the possibility when applying to colleges, and will need to start planning their courses accordingly several years ahead of time.

Reserve Officer Training Corps (ROTC)

The good old ROTC has branches at many colleges. To qualify for ROTC scholarships you generally need to apply to the program early in the senior year of high school. Competition for these awards is tough, but if a student is selected he or she will receive a full or partial scholarship plus a $100-per-month allowance. The catch, of course, is that the student has to join the military for four years of active duty plus two more years on reserve. While on active duty, many students are allowed to go to graduate school on full scholarship. A student can join a ROTC program once he or she entered college, but will not necessarily get a scholarship.

Qualifications for four-year scholarships depend on the military branch; for the Army, students (male and female) must have a GPA of at least 2.5, an SAT score of 1000 (out of 1600) or an ACT score of 19, they must pass a physical, and they must also impress an interviewer.

Service Academies

The service academies (the U.S. Military Academy at West Point and the U.S. Naval Academy at Annapolis are probably the best known) are extremely difficult to get into. Good grades are essential, as is a recommendation from a senator or a member of Congress. However, all this trouble may be worth it, for the service academies have a great reputation for the quality of their programs and they are absolutely free. Again, in exchange for this education, a student must agree to serve as an officer in the armed forces for several years.

Wacky Jobs students have held during (or via) college

Costume Lending Assistant

Great Worms Project Research Assistant

Psychology Test Subject

Prayer Chat Line Operator

Lab Rat Monitor

Jobs

Whether your aid package included federal work-study or not, a part-time job is always an option for making ends meet (this works in the real world, too!) Work-study guarantees a fair rate and hours, but there are plenty of other equally good jobs that can be found either through the campus career office, message/bulletin boards, or just plain old pounding the pavement or Craig's List.

More than 70 percent of students work part-time at some point in their college career, typically a modest number of hours (around ten hours a week). While there's always going to be spot gigs and flexible shifts (like in food service) that are meant for college students, you can also try to kill two birds with one stone and find a job that might pad the resume or lead into a full-time position after college, such as assisting a professor with research, or working at a low level in a company.

Innovative Payment and Loan Options

The very best type of loans, as we've said before, are the government-subsidized student loans, followed by the various other need- and non-need-based loans detailed in Step 7. However, there are still a few fringe scenarios surrounding loans.

Loans Forgiven

A few colleges have programs under which some of your student loans may be forgiven if you meet certain conditions. At Cornell University, for example, Tradition Fellows, who hold jobs while they are in college, are given awards that replace their student loans by up to $4,000 per year in acknowledgment of their work ethic. Even federal loans can be forgiven under certain circumstances. Head Start, Peace Corps, or VISTA volunteers may not have to repay all of their federal loans, for example.

Descriptions of requirements for loan forgiveness through Americorps, Peace Corps, VISTA

Loan Forgiveness Terms for Americorps, Volunteers in Service to America (VISTA), and Peace Corps Volunteers

Work full-time at an eligible nonprofit or government agency while making steady student loan payments for ten years (120 monthly payments, not necessarily consecutive), and the federal government will forgive the balance of your student loans. If loans are being paid under an Income-Based Repayment, then these payments may be very small (as little as $5 per month).

Additionally, Americorps and VISTA volunteers can earn stipends and educational awards that are to be used specifically for loans.

Moral Obligation Loans

This one's going to seem made up, but it is a 100 percent true option at some schools (such as Kenyon College): the college makes a loan to the student, and the student agrees to pay back the loan. That's it. There is no legal obligation to pay back the money. The student has a moral obligation to repay.

Several schools have decided to try this, and the results, of course, won't be in for some time. At the moment, when a student repays the loan, the repayment is considered a tax-deductible charitable contribution. The IRS probably won't still have that loophole in for long, but nevertheless, this is a wonderful deal because it allows the student flexibility in deciding when to pay the loan back, and does not affect the child's credit rating. On the off chance your college is offering this option, grab it.

What is Tuition Refund Insurance?

A tuition refund insurance policy is designed to protect the parent if the student is forced to withdraw in the middle of a term. Most colleges give partial refunds when a student has to withdraw (the amount depends on how far into the term, as well as school policies).

For an insurance premium of normally $150 to $400 per academic year, you can have peace of mind that any non-refunded payments for tuition and possibly room & board are not a total loss. Parents can be refunded up to 100 percent of the difference for what the college doesn't refund for medically-related withdrawals, and some policies also offer coverage if the student is forced to withdraw for other reasons—such as a death in the family or an employment-related relocation of the parents. Check with the FAO or the student billing office for availability at the college of your choice.

Short-Term Prepayment

Recently, some colleges have been touting tuition prepayment as the answer to everything. In the short-term version of tuition prepayment, the parent pays the college the entire four years' worth of tuition (room and board are typically excluded) sometime just before the student begins their first year. The college "locks in" the tuition rate for the entire four years. Regardless of how much tuition rises during the four years, the parent will not owe any more toward tuition.

The rub here is that since most parents don't have four years of tuition on hand, some colleges will lend it to them or parents can, for example, remortgage their home for the proceeds. The parents pay back the loan with interest over a set time period. The colleges love this arrangement, because it allows them to make a nice profit if the market is strong. If the parents can afford to pay the entire amount without borrowing, then the colleges invest your money in taxable investments, which they don't have to pay taxes on (since they're tax-exempt). Whatever course you pursue, the revenue the colleges earn from these prepayment plans usually makes up for any tuition increases.

> ### Is Prepayment a Good Idea for the Parent?
>
> Avoiding tuition increases each year sounds like a sure thing, but any possible savings depend on what interest rates are doing. If you would have to borrow the money to make the prepayment, the question is whether your after-tax cost of borrowing will be less than the tuition increases over the four years. If so, prepayment may make sense. Unless interest rates are extremely low and will remain so over the time the student is in college, prepayment may end up costing you more money than paying as you go.

Payment Plans and Financing Options

Many families have difficulty coming up with their Family Contribution in one lump sum each semester. There are a number of commercial organizations that will assist you with spreading the payment out over time (a nominal fee is usually charged); many schools have their own deferred payment plans as well. Some of these programs are financing plans that charge interest and involve repayment over a number of years; others are simply payment plans in which you make monthly payments.

The college financial aid office or bursar's (student billing) office should be able to provide you with information regarding all your payment options, as well as the names of those commercial plans (if any) that can be used at their school. Be sure to read the fine print before you sign up for any of these programs.

A Few Hundred Thousand Pennies Saved

Congratulations, dear parent and student, you've made it to the end!

Hopefully the financial aid process has been demystified, and this book got to you with enough time for you to begin planning for the process ahead, and for the student to know in advance what they'll need to do for their part. Remember— while most families do end up getting need-based aid, most also end up borrowing money as well. The key is to maximize the amount of aid your family can receive, and then minimize the costs of paying off the rest.

Our intent here was to give the parent and child an understanding of the aid process and some idea of the possibilities for controlling that process, but this book is by no means encyclopedic, and the rules change almost constantly. You've got all of the basic information at hand, and a good financial planner can take you the rest of the way there.

From the time you submit the first FAFSA until the student flips that graduation cap tassel, money is going to be on your mind, but at least you'll know you've done all you could to lessen that load. Good luck!

INDEX

D

E

F

G

I

L

M

O

P

Q

R

S

T

U

V

W

NOTES

NOTES

NOTES

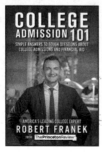